RENEWING  WORSHIP

Daily Prayer

Evangelical Lutheran Church in America
Published by Augsburg Fortress

RENEWING WORSHIP 7
Daily Prayer

This resource has been prepared by the Evangelical Lutheran Church in America for provisional use.

Copyright © 2004 Evangelical Lutheran Church in America.

Published by Augsburg Fortress, Publishers. All rights reserved. Except for brief quotations in critical articles or reviews and for uses described in the following paragraph, no part of this book may be reproduced in any manner without prior written permission from the publisher. Contact: Permissions, Augsburg Fortress, Box 1209, Minneapolis MN 55440-1209, (800) 421-0239.

Except as noted on specific music items, permission is granted to reproduce the material on pages i–192 for use in worship and study, provided that no part of the reproduction is for sale, copies are for onetime local use, and the following copyright notice appears: From *Daily Prayer,* copyright © 2004, administered by Augsburg Fortress. May be reproduced by permission for use only between October 1, 2004 and December 31, 2006.

The paper used in this publication meets the minimum requirements of American National Standard for Information Sciences—Permanence of Paper for Printed Library Materials, ANSI Z329.48-1984.

Manufactured in the U.S.A. ISBN 0-8066-7007-X

08 07 06 05 04   1   2   3   4   5

Contents

iv   Preface

vi   Introduction

1   Daily Prayer
Shape of the Rite   3
Evening Prayer   6
Morning Prayer   12
Night Prayer   18
Supplemental Materials   24
Pattern and Examples for Personal and Small Group Prayer   28

39   Psalms for Daily Prayer
Examples of Approaches to Psalm Translation   40

63   Daily Lectionary

101   Service Music

182   Acknowledgments

184   Index

186   Evaluation

Preface

In the years since the publication of *Lutheran Book of Worship* in 1978, the pace of change both within the church and beyond has quickened. The past three decades have seen not only areas of growing ecumenical consensus but also a deepened focus on the church's mission to the world. The church has embraced broadened understandings of culture, increasing musical diversity, changes in the usage of language, a renewed understanding of the central pattern of Christian worship, and an explosion of electronic media and technologies. These shifts have had a profound effect on the weekly assembly gathered around word and sacrament. The present situation calls for a renewal of worship and of common resources for worship, a renewal grounded in the treasures of the church's history while open to the possibilities of the future.

Renewing Worship is a response to these emerging changes in the life of the church and the world. Renewing Worship includes a series of provisional resources intended to provide worship leaders with a range of proposed strategies and materials that address the various liturgical and musical needs of the church. These resources are offered to assist the renewal of corporate worship in a variety of settings, especially among Lutheran churches, in anticipation of the next generation of primary worship resources.

Published beginning in 2001, this series includes hymns and songs (newly written or discovered as well as new approaches to common texts and tunes), liturgical texts and music for weekly and seasonal use, occasional rites (such as marriage, healing, and funeral), resources for daily prayer (morning prayer, evening prayer, and night prayer), psalms and canticles, prayers and propers related to the lectionary, and other supporting materials. Over the course of several years, worship leaders have the opportunity to obtain and evaluate a wide range of Renewing Worship resources both in traditional print format and in electronic form delivered via the Internet (www.renewingworship.org).

These published resources, however, are only one component of the Renewing Worship multiyear plan led by the Evangelical Lutheran Church in America (ELCA) as it enters the next generation of its worship life. Endorsed by the ELCA Church Council and carried out in partnership by the ELCA Division for Congregational Ministries and the Publishing House of the ELCA (Augsburg Fortress), this plan for worship renewal includes five components. The first phase (2001–2002) is a consultative process intended to develop principles for language, music, preaching, and worship space. Related to the ELCA's statement on sacramental practices, *The Use of the Means of Grace*, the outcome of the 2001–2002 consultative process has been published as *Principles for Worship*. These principles are intended to undergird future worship resource development and encourage congregational study, response, and practice.

The second phase (2001–2005) includes a series of editorial teams that collect, develop, and revise worship materials for provisional use. The liturgical and musical resource proposals that emerge from the editorial teams are being published during the third phase of this plan (also in 2001–2005) as trial-use resources in the Renewing Worship series, including the present volume, *Daily Prayer.* These materials include proposals for newly developed, ecumenically shared, or recently revised texts, rites, and music. Crucial to this phase will be careful evaluation and response by congregations and worship leaders based on these proposed strategies and provisional materials.

The fourth phase of the plan includes regional conferences for conversation, resource introduction and evaluation, and congregational feedback. The final phase of the process (2005 and beyond) envisions the drafting of a comprehensive proposal for new primary worship resources designed to succeed *Lutheran Book of Worship.*

As the plan progresses, the shape and parameters of that proposal continue to unfold. The goal, however, will remain constant: renewing the worship of God in the church as it carries out Christ's mission in a new day.

Introduction

Daily Prayer, the seventh resource in the Renewing Worship series, focuses on patterns of prayer linked to the rhythms of the day and of daily life—whether this praying takes place in the gathered Christian assembly, in small groups reflecting a variety of contexts, or in the life of the individual Christian. An annotated shape of the rite outlines an overarching pattern for daily prayer and illustrates the way this pattern unfolds at three times when communal prayer has long been observed: evening, morning, and at night. Provisional texts for general assembly use are provided for rites at these three times. In addition, several examples are offered to model ways in which the patterns might be realized for the gatherings of smaller groups or for household use. Rounding out the body of provisional texts are samples of various psalm translations for review and evaluation, as well as an excerpt from a proposed daily lectionary that is related to the three-year Sunday lectionary.

In addition to the provisional textual material, this resource includes samples of music for the rites, some of it newly composed. These service music options are presented in a separate section from which worship planners can select appropriate choices.

It is important to emphasize that this volume is not a complete collection of the texts and liturgical music to be proposed for daily prayer in the worship resources that will replace *Lutheran Book of Worship (LBW).* This provisional volume includes mostly a sampling of new materials offered for testing and evaluation. Longer-term core resources will include also some materials carried over from current usage. Feedback from congregations about existing materials and response to these newly proposed materials will help determine the balance between "new" and "old" that will be recommended for more lasting resources.

An essential foundation for all Renewing Worship resources is *The Use of the Means of Grace,* the statement on the practice of word and sacrament adopted for guidance and practice by the Evangelical Lutheran Church in America in 1997.[1] Some highlights from that statement are noted in the following introduction, but the statement's intent and spirit are best captured by a careful study of the original. In addition to *The Use of the Means of Grace,* the churchwide consultative work that resulted in the 2002 release of *Principles for Worship* has provided guidance and support for the work on these provisional materials.[2]

DAILY PRAYER: PRAYING WITHOUT CEASING

Daily prayer has sometimes been related to the New Testament admonition to "pray without ceasing . . . for this is the will of God in Christ Jesus for you."[3] This encouragement may seem impossible until it is placed in the context of scripture's many reflections on the life of prayer. These suggest that daily prayer is but one dimension of living every day in relationship with God, with the church, and with the neighbor—a relationship that is marked at various times by conversation, entreaty, listening, responding, waiting, watching,

---

[1] *The Use of the Means of Grace: A Statement on the Practice of Word and Sacrament* (Chicago: Evangelical Lutheran Church in America, 1997).
[2] *Principles for Worship,* Renewing Worship, vol. 2 (Minneapolis: Augsburg Fortress, 2002).
[3] 1 Thessalonians 5:17-18.

even wrestling with God. Although the daily prayer of the Christian may include specific texts like "Come, Lord Jesus" at meals or the Lord's Prayer, daily prayer more broadly includes such dimensions as an active reflection on one's daily activities in the context of faith and a conscious determination to bring the needs of the whole world into the presence of God.

"Praying without ceasing" is also an apt description for the activity of the whole people of God at many times and in many places around the world. A hymnwriter expressed it this way: "As to each continent and island the dawn leads on another day, the voice of prayer is never silent."[4] The daily prayer of the Christian, whether alone or with others, is always enfolded in and amplified by the prayer of many other sisters and brothers and communities of faith. The use of some common patterns and elements for daily prayer is one way of highlighting this global linkage of Christians at prayer.

DAILY PRAYER: HOLY CONVERSATION

Martin Luther once concisely described prayer and worship as "holy conversation": God speaking the living and saving word, the church replying in song and prayer.[5] This holy conversation extends beyond a bilateral relationship between God and the people of God to encompass also the neighbor, the whole world. This dimension is present also in the primary weekly assembly through such elements as proclamation, intercessory prayer, and the sending, but daily prayer in the midst of the world is another important place in which the needs of the whole creation are voiced. Daily prayer sounds the cry of all creation—a joyful cry of praise, a groaning cry of lament—into the ears of God as part of this holy conversation. Whether one person or a community is praying, the prayer participates in a more universal prayer.

From this perspective daily prayer is not merely an exercise that is good for spiritual health. Prayer is an invitation for God to re-orient the individual, the community of faith, the society, the culture, and the world to God's own vision for all creation.

DAILY PRAYER AND THE MEANS OF GRACE

Daily prayer, whether personal or corporate, flows from the assembly of God's people around word and sacrament. Prayer on each day of the week carries forth and prepares for the primary gathering on the first day of the week. The psalms, prayers, and readings for each day deepen through and over time the feast of word and meal, and in turn the Sunday celebration deepens the daily round of prayer.

The daily re-appropriation of the gifts of God in word and sacrament is an important theme in Martin Luther's writings. Daily prayer, for Luther, was the daily opportunity to be nourished by the word of God and turn to God in prayer for help and support, for guidance, for forgiveness, and for understanding—the ongoing benefits of baptism itself.

---

[4] John Ellerton, "The day you gave us, Lord, has ended," *Lutheran Book of Worship* 274.
[5] Martin Luther, "Sermon at the Dedication of the Castle Church in Torgau," in *Luther's Works,* vol. 51, 333.

For not only do we daily need God's Word just as we do our daily bread; we also must have it every day in order to stand against the daily and incessant attacks and ambushes of the devil with his thousand arts.[6]

Daily prayer calls the people of God back to baptism and sends them forth renewed in their baptismal vows. The prayerful reminder of baptism is the meditation on the daily dying and rising with Christ—thus Luther's encouragement to make the sign of the cross each morning—as well as the unceasing call to be what God has fashioned, a community, a holy communion.[7]

DAILY PRAYER AND THE CHRISTIAN ASSEMBLY

Although daily prayer encompasses much more than the orders of service prayed by the gathered Christian assembly, the provisional materials in this volume give particular focus to assembly patterns and rites, since these are more likely to be a part of future core worship resources. These materials acknowledge that "assemblies for worship are not limited to Sunday or to celebrations of Word and Sacrament. Christians gather for worship on other days of the week, for morning or evening prayer. . . . The communal observance of morning and evening prayer . . . [is an] appropriate tradition."[8]

The patterns of communal daily prayer are rooted in scripture and shaped over the centuries by the liturgy of the hours, the daily prayer traditions of the church. From its beginnings the church sought to hallow God and to sanctify time by regularly and intentionally gathering for prayer throughout the day and night. Over the years methods for praying the round of psalms daily, weekly, and monthly were drawn up along with fitting hymns and forms of prayer. The church year has provided further organization, including commemorations of faithful women and men through the ages, and an orderly way to celebrate the great story of God's saving work in Christ.

These communal prayers are more encompassing than the individual's and provide the necessary balance to the individual's prayers, lest they become narrow and unrelated to the needs of others. Evening prayer, morning prayer, and prayer at night are the times for which common liturgies have been provided in recent Lutheran practice, and forms of these are provided in this volume as well. Although few communities have been able to observe a full round of daily communal prayer, many have observed two, or three, or five days with some regularity, such as college and seminary communities, deaconess communities, denominational administrative offices, neighborhood prayer and Bible study groups, and the like. Congregations have often observed daily prayer on a seasonal basis, such as midweek services during Lent and Advent, although some have also used morning prayer as a non-eucharistic option on Sunday. More recently, some congregations have offered monthly or weekly services of contemplative prayer, using resources such as those originating in the Taizé Community.

---

[6] The Large Catechism, Preface, *Book of Concord,* ed. Robert Kolb and Timothy J. Wengert (Minneapolis: Fortress, 2000), 381–82.
[7] The Small Catechism, *Book of Concord,* 363.
[8] *The Use of the Means of Grace,* principle 13, application 13A.

In a 24/7 world, the church also is becoming aware that daily patterns of living are not always in sync with the historic patterns of prayer. New rhythms of faith communities may well suggest new patterns of praying, too. For example, those who work night shifts might find it odd to pray morning prayer to begin their "day," for the sun has set and darkness covers their hours of waking and work. Those who work at night also know the difficulty of being a part of a congregation with a typical worship schedule. Might the Jewish marking of time, beginning the day at sundown, call forth images and patterns of prayer for those who work at night—often in service to others? It is more difficult to provide general, communal orders of prayer that address the many varying contexts congregations face. The examples in this resource of shaping daily prayer patterns to a number of particular contexts—meetings of church groups, Christians gathering in the workplace—are only a suggested beginning toward ways that congregations and Christians in their own contexts can adapt communal forms of prayer.

DAILY PRAYER—GUIDE TO THIS RESOURCE

This resource presents provisional materials for daily prayer, focused on the church's gathering in assembly for these liturgies, but including also examples of how daily prayer may unfold in smaller groups and in personal use. These materials include the following:

- *Daily Prayer in Common—Shape of the Rite:* a brief description of a fundamental common pattern for daily prayer, illustrating also the variations in the ways evening prayer, morning prayer, and night prayer reflect this pattern.

- *Evening Prayer, Morning Prayer, Night Prayer:* text-only presentations of the rites proposed for assembly use, so that these can be seen and evaluated apart from the musical settings of some of these texts.

- *Supplemental Materials:* a section of alternative texts for elements of the liturgy, in addition to the few that appear in the rites. Included here are seasonal dialogs for the service of light in evening prayer; two additional prayers of thanksgiving for light; seasonal antiphons (invitatories) for the first psalm at morning prayer; an additional model for the praying section of morning prayer; and an alternative remembrance of baptism for morning prayer (a paschal blessing).

- *Pattern and Examples for Personal and Small Group Prayer:* a narrative describing how the fundamental pattern for daily prayer may be fleshed out in situations other than the worshiping assembly is followed by four examples that illustrate a few specific ways that this might happen.

- *Approaches to Psalm Translation:* a sampling of psalms illustrating several approaches to the question of psalm translation. Some of these psalms, with a variety of systems for musical pointing, are available at www.renewingworship.org.

▶ *Daily Lectionary Related to the Revised Common Lectionary:* a small section of scripture readings suitable for daily prayer and related to the Sunday readings, chosen for the period from Advent to Pentecost in year A (2005). These readings are from a draft of a three-year cycle of readings presently being developed by the Consultation on Common Texts.

▶ *Service Music:* settings of the primary psalms and canticles for evening prayer and morning prayer. Included for evening prayer are several settings or paraphrases of the light hymn (Phos hilaron); Psalm 141; and the gospel canticle, the Magnificat. Included for morning prayer are several settings of Psalm 95:1-7a (Venite); the gospel canticle (Benedictus); and the alternate gospel canticle (Te Deum). The musical settings in this part of the resource are only a sample to illustrate the range of possibilities for singing these significant portions of daily prayer.

DEVELOPMENTS IN THE PROPOSED RITES FOR DAILY PRAYER

The careful work done in the preparation of the daily prayer materials for *LBW* has by and large been retained. The proposals in this volume include several aspects of continuing development, which are highlighted below. (Some additional materials are still in preparation, including responsive prayer and the great litany.)

A fundamental and natural *pattern* or *shape* for daily prayer is identified, in order to make more transparent the simple architecture and progression of these rites. The proposals reflect a relatively parallel structure for the three assembly forms of daily prayer, consisting of Opening, Psalm and Song, Word, and Praying. An increased number of options, however, allow for great flexibility in the ways the rites may be enacted.

Even though evening prayer and morning prayer center in praise, reflection upon the scriptures, and praying for the world, they are also at times the occasion for brief preaching or other proclamation. These rites propose that *the natural place for proclamation is in proximity to the reading of scripture,* rather than in a separate preaching office appended to the rite. (Night prayer is a simpler rite that includes only a brief reading of scripture.)

It is proposed that psalms and canticles from the Bible normally be used on their own, *without the addition of a doxology,* in order to acknowledge the integrity and completeness of these texts. *LBW* implemented this principle with respect to the psalms; here the principle is applied also to the gospel canticles. Psalm prayers will eventually be provided for the psalms, but their use is proposed to be optional, so that those who wish may allow silent devotional reflection to be an adequate and complete response to these songs from the Hebrew scriptures.

While recognizing the broad ecumenical character of daily prayer, it is proposed that at several places the *resources of the Lutheran tradition be given greater prominence.* For example, Luther's Morning Prayer and Evening Prayer are here included as optional conclusions to the praying section (the second prayer in each set), and the proposed morning prayer rite incorporates Luther's encouragement of the remembrance of baptism each morning by making it an optional part of the opening section.

As in *LBW*, the proposed rites for daily prayer *do not require a pastor for leadership,* and in fact leadership by lay persons is encouraged. All the texts, including the blessings, are presented to reflect this principle.

Musical forms will eventually be provided so that the assembly rites may be sung. With the exception of the gospel canticles, *most of the psalm and canticle texts are not placed within the rite,* in order to accommodate the range of approaches to text and music that may be used and that are suggested in the service music section.

Several *alternative texts* are provided in the rites or in supplemental materials: in evening prayer, dialogs and thanksgivings for light; in morning prayer, a second opening dialog that includes a doxology from the Byzantine tradition; in night prayer, several additional brief scripture readings and an alternate opening sentence and blessing.

As mentioned earlier, the proposal for morning prayer suggests an intentional *remembrance of baptism,* in keeping with Luther's catechetical suggestions that each morning Christians recall their baptism by making the sign of the cross, and further that in baptism the old self is daily drowned and the new self daily comes forth and rises.[9] The remembrance may be extend to a visible and tangible sign, such as sprinkling the assembly with water. The *paschal blessing,* introduced to Lutherans in *LBW,* is an alternative way of remembering baptism at the conclusion of morning prayer, especially fitting on Sundays and festival days.

Both currently-used translations of the Lord's Prayer are included in this proposal. Although in many places among Lutherans a generation has grown up knowing only the newer ecumenical version, it seems premature to propose that it be presented exclusively given the continuing widespread use of the older version.

This set of proposals is intended to encourage *greater flexibility in shaping daily prayer for various contexts and circumstances.* Rather than providing a single way of abbreviating the assembly rites, a number of examples are offered to illustrate the ways in which local worship leaders might shape and contextualize the resources for daily prayer.

Scripture reading continues to have a central role in these rites. This proposal includes an excerpt from a daily lectionary project that is currently in progress by the Consultation on Common Texts. It is proposed that, as an alternative to a daily lectionary system that involves reading the Bible in sequence, *a daily lectionary related to the Sunday readings* might be a more practical approach for many communities, especially those that do not meet every day, morning and evening, to follow a sequential pattern of reading. This

---

[9] Small Catechism, *Book of Concord,* 363, 360.

Sunday lectionary-related approach proposes that the readings for Thursday through Saturday prepare for and anticipate the Sunday lectionary readings, and that the readings for Monday through Wednesday reflect upon the previous Sunday. Communities that gather more occasionally during the week may feel free to select from the whole body of readings related to a Sunday, not merely those assigned to a particular day.

MUSIC FOR DAILY PRAYER

Included in this resource is a small selection of music to support assembly rites of evening and morning prayer. Several newly commissioned works are a part of this section. A basic accompaniment for these materials is included in this resource. A musical setting of night prayer is also in preparation.

USING THIS RESOURCE

This collection is intended for provisional use among congregations of the Evangelical Lutheran Church in America and beyond. Worship leaders are encouraged to consider a congregation's history and worship practices before introducing new materials.

Materials in this collection are designed for provisional use in worship. Electronic files of selected materials are available for download (www.renewingworship.org) and placement in congregational worship folders.

QUESTIONS OF COPYRIGHT

As a whole, the texts, music, and arrangement of materials in *Daily Prayer* are covered under the copyright of this publication or are used here by arrangement with other copyright holders. Some individual items may be in the public domain. The acknowledgments section contains details about the sources.

Limited permission is granted to reproduce provisional texts and most of the provisional music (except as noted on specific service music items) for local congregational use in worship and study, provided that no part of the reproduction is for sale, copies are for local use, and the following copyright notice appears: From *Daily Prayer,* copyright © 2004, administered by Augsburg Fortress. May be reproduced by permission for use only between October 1, 2004 and December 31, 2006.

EVALUATION

An essential goal of Renewing Worship is the evaluation of strategies and content proposals by worshiping congregations and their leaders. Included in each printed volume as well as on the Web site (www.renewingworship.org) is an evaluation form that addresses the strategies employed in each volume of the series. Feedback received will help to shape the subsequent stages of the process toward new worship materials.

… RENEWING WORSHIP …

Daily Prayer

Shape of the Rite
Daily Prayer in Common

From the gathering around word and sacrament on the first day of the week, Christians are sent by God to continue their worship each day through lives of service. St. Paul's guidance to "pray without ceasing . . . for this is the will of God in Christ Jesus for you" (1 Thess. 5:17-18) suggests that the Christian life *is* prayer: a continuous openness to the presence of God, an ongoing responsiveness to the word of God, a constant recognition that all of life is in Christ, and a daily engagement in care for one another, for all those in need, and for the whole creation.

Daily prayer in common is a gift that nourishes growth toward living all of daily life in such a posture of prayer. The church provides patterns for prayer at particular times of the day in order to encourage a structure and regularity to daily prayer, so that Christians may build one another up in a life of faith—although the daily prayers of God's people, alone or gathered, are not limited to these patterns. Whether one prays as part of a larger assembly, in a smaller group where two or three are gathered, or through one's own personal prayer, each member of Christ's body is praying in common with the whole church. Punctuating daily life, times of focused prayer assist God's people in receiving all of time as a gift.

Evening and morning have long been the primary times for common prayer in a number of faith traditions, acknowledging the gifts of creation and of time. For Christians these times for prayer have an additional, paschal dimension—calling to mind Christ's passage through death to resurrection. As evening comes, Christians look to the light of Christ; they remember the blessed night when Jesus was raised from death; and they entrust themselves and the whole world into the hands of God, anticipating the great awakening of the resurrection to eternal life. With the rising sun, Christians praise God for the resurrection of Jesus Christ; they daily return to the waters of baptism through which they have died and been raised to new life with Christ; and they ask the Holy Spirit's help in taking up the cross to follow Jesus into another day.

Night prayer (prayer at the close of the day) is an additional time for common prayer that has deep roots and meaning, offering a time to examine and confess the sins of the day, while entrusting the hours of sleep into God's hands. In the present time, the fact that the rhythms of the day are not the same for everyone calls for the exploration of patterns of prayer that may be used across a variety of times and contexts.

Although the patterns for these times of common daily prayer are not uniform, they reveal a natural arc of movement and a number of common features: *psalm and song,* grounded in the oldest hymnbook of the faithful; *word,* the reading and reflection upon the scriptures; and *praying,* which can take a variety of forms, often bringing to God particular concerns and joys of the community, the world, or one's own daily life. This core pattern is often preceded by an *opening,* whether brief or extended, and typically concludes with a word of blessing.

OPENING

Evening	Morning	Night
Dialog	Dialog	Dialog
Light Hymn	Remembrance of Baptism	Night Hymn
Thanksgiving for Light		Confession
		Peace

The patterns of daily prayer may begin with words and songs that acknowledge the church's opening of hearts and voices to the presence of God. The beginning of morning prayer recognizes that even this opening is itself the gift of God: "O Lord, open my lips, and my mouth shall proclaim your praise" (Ps. 51:15). The opening may be extended with a hymn and action linked to the time of day: thanksgiving for the Light that is Christ, at evening; remembrance of baptism, in the morning; confession of sin, at night.

PSALM AND SONG

Evening	Morning	Night
Psalm 141 or 121	**Psalm 95 or 63 or 100**	**Psalm 4 or 91 or 134**
and/or others	and/or others	and/or others
Hymn/Song	Hymn/Song	Hymn/Song

Singing the psalms is a primary element of daily prayer. The Psalter, the 150 psalms of the Bible, has long been at the heart of daily praying: in the gospels their words are often on Jesus' lips, and Christians through the centuries have prayed them daily. Martin Luther considered the psalms the summary of all scripture, speaking concretely and eloquently to many situations, and allowing the realistic expression of a wide range of human response, including questioning and anger as well as hope and faith. The psalms include expressions of adoration, praise, thanksgiving for God's deliverance, lament, confession, intercession, teaching—often more than one of these within a single psalm. Used in the context of prayer, they are at the same time God's words to us and our response to God. These foundational songs may be complemented with other songs from the church's treasury, such as hymns that reflect the time of day or the season of the church's year.

Central elements of the liturgy are noted in bold letters; other elements support and reveal the essential shape of Christian worship.

WORD

Evening	*Morning*	*Night*
Reading(s)	**Reading(s)**	**Reading**
Reflection	Reflection	Reflection
Gospel Canticle	Gospel Canticle	Gospel Canticle

Although singing and praying the psalms is already an encounter with the word of God, the church's daily prayer provides for the reading of other parts of the Bible beyond the psalms. Daily lectionaries offer useful structures for reading the scriptures over several years, or in relationship to the Sunday readings, especially within evening prayer and morning prayer. The suggested readings in night prayer are typically brief, a verse or two for meditation as the day comes to a close. Reflection upon the reading(s) may take one or more of a variety of forms: a time of silence, response through music or other art forms, or a brief form of verbal interpretation such as preaching, teaching, or personal witness. As a further part of the encounter with God's word, the forms of daily prayer commend the use of gospel canticles, foundational New Testament songs: the song of Mary ("My soul proclaims the greatness of the Lord") in evening prayer, the song of Zechariah ("Blessed are you, Lord") in morning prayer, and the song of Simeon ("Now, Lord, you let your servant go") in night prayer. With these songs the church both proclaims and hears the liberating gospel.

PRAYING

Evening	*Morning*	*Night*
Litany	**Prayers**	**Prayers**
Lord's Prayer	**Lord's Prayer**	**Lord's Prayer**
Blessing	Blessing	Blessing
Peace	Peace	

Although in one sense everything the church does in daily prayer is "praying," the patterns for daily prayer include a central element that engages the people of God in praying in more specific and contextual ways, especially through intercession—not only for their own needs but the needs of others, for healing, for justice, for enemies, for the creation, for peace, for the sick and the dying, for the reign of God. These prayers make clear that the Christian's prayerful relationship with God is always also a passionate connection with the world God has made. All these prayers are gathered up in the praying of the Lord's Prayer, itself given as a model for all prayer. The patterns for common daily prayer conclude simply, with a word of blessing. The blessing may be followed by the sharing of a sign of peace (at night prayer, the peace may follow the confession).

EVENING PRAYER *Vespers*

OPENING

DIALOG

Evening prayer may begin with a dialog between leader and assembly. During the dialog, a large, lighted candle may be carried to its stand in the assembly.

A
Jesus Christ is the Light of the world,
the light no darkness can overcome.

Stay with us, Lord, for it is evening,
and the day is almost over.

Let your light scatter the darkness,
and illumine your church.

B *pp. 24–25* ▶
God is our light and our salvation,
our refuge and our stronghold.

From the rising of the sun to its setting,
we praise your name, O God.

For with you is the fountain of life,
and in your light we see light.

If the light hymn and thanksgiving for light are omitted, the liturgy continues with the psalmody on p. 7.

LIGHT HYMN *R401–R404* ▶

"Joyous Light of glory" or another appropriate hymn may be sung, during which other candles may be lighted. When the large candle is used, other candles are lighted from its flame.

THANKSGIVING FOR LIGHT

The leader and the assembly give thanks for the gift of created light and for the light of Christ.
The Lord be with you.
And also with you.

Let us give thanks to the Lord our God.
It is right to give our thanks and praise.

A *p. 25* ▶
We give you thanks, O God,
for in the beginning you called forth light by your Word,
and you set lights in the sky to govern night and day.
In a pillar of cloud by day and a pillar of fire by night
you led your people into freedom.

Lighten our darkness, we pray.
Let your Word, Jesus Christ,
be a lamp to our feet and a light to our path.

Honor and praise to you, merciful God,
for you love your whole creation,
and with all your creatures we give you glory,
through your Son Jesus Christ,
in the unity of the Holy Spirit, now and forever.
Amen.

PSALM AND SONG

PSALM

R405–R409 ▶

The psalmody begins with Psalm 141, Psalm 121, or another psalm appropriate for evening.

A time of silence follows. A psalm prayer may conclude the silence.

The psalmody may continue with one or more additional psalms. Each is followed by a time of silence, which may be concluded by a psalm prayer.

SONG

Additional assembly song may follow the psalmody, such as a hymn appropriate to the time of day or the season.

WORD

READINGS

One or more readings from scripture are proclaimed. Each reading may be concluded:

A	B
Holy wisdom, holy word.	The word of the Lord.
Thanks be to God.	**Thanks be to God.**

REFLECTION

The reading of scripture is followed by silence for reflection and meditation. Other forms of reflection may also follow, such as brief commentary, teaching, or personal witness; non-biblical readings; interpretation through music or other art forms; or guided conversation among those present.

The reflection may conclude with these or similar words:

A
The word is near you,
on your lips and in your heart.
**Everyone who calls on the name
of the Lord shall be saved.**

B
You have been born anew
through the living and abiding word of God.

GOSPEL CANTICLE   R410–R413 ▶

The gospel canticle for evening is the song of Mary (the Magnificat):

My soul proclaims the greatness of the Lord,
my spirit rejoices in God my Savior,
for you, Lord, have looked with favor on your lowly servant.
From this day all generations will call me blessed:
    you, the Almighty, have done great things for me,
    and holy is your name.
    You have mercy on those who fear you,
    from generation to generation.
You have shown strength with your arm
and scattered the proud in their conceit,
casting down the mighty from their thrones
and lifting up the lowly.
You have filled the hungry with good things
and sent the rich away empty.
You have come to the aid of your servant Israel,
to remember the promise of mercy,
the promise made to our forebears,
to Abraham and his children forever.

PRAYING

The leader and the assembly join in prayers of intercession and thanksgiving. The following litany or another form of the prayers may be used. The prayers conclude with the Lord's Prayer.

LITANY   R414–R416 ▶

In peace, let us pray to the Lord.
Lord, have mercy.

For the peace from above, and for our salvation,
let us pray to the Lord.
Lord, have mercy.

For the peace of the whole world,
for the well-being of the church of God,
and for the unity of all,
let us pray to the Lord.
Lord, have mercy.

For this holy house,
and for all who offer here their worship and praise,
let us pray to the Lord.
Lord, have mercy.

For the health of the creation,
for abundant harvests that all may share,
and for peaceful times,
let us pray to the Lord.
Lord, have mercy.

For public servants, the government, and those who protect us;
for those who work to bring peace, justice, healing, and protection
in this and every place,
let us pray to the Lord.
Lord, have mercy.

For those who travel,
for those who are sick and suffering,
and for those who are in captivity,
let us pray to the Lord.
Lord, have mercy.

For deliverance in the time of affliction, wrath, danger, and need,
let us pray to the Lord.
Lord, have mercy.

For *names* and all servants of the church,
for this assembly,
and for all people who await from the Lord great and abundant mercy,
let us pray to the Lord.
Lord, have mercy.

Other petitions may be added.

Help, save, comfort, and defend us, gracious Lord.

A time of silence follows.

Giving thanks for all who have gone before us and are at rest,
rejoicing in the communion of (*names* and) all the saints,
we commend ourselves, one another, and our whole life to you,
through Jesus Christ our Lord.
Amen.   *or*   **To you, O Lord.**

CONCLUDING PRAYER

A
O God,
you have called your servants to ventures
of which we cannot see the ending,
by paths as yet untrodden,
through perils unknown.
Give us faith to go out with good courage,
not knowing where we go,
but only that your hand is leading us
and your love supporting us;
through Jesus Christ our Lord.
Amen.

B
We give thanks to you, heavenly Father,
through Jesus Christ your dear Son,
that you have this day so graciously protected us.
We ask you to forgive us all our sins
and the wrong we have done.
By your great mercy defend us
from the perils and dangers of this night.
Into your hands we commend
our bodies and souls and all that is ours.
Let your holy angels have charge of us,
that the wicked one have no power over us.
Amen.

C
O God,
from whom come all holy desires,
all good counsels, and all just works:
give to us, your servants,
that peace which the world cannot give,
that our hearts may be set to obey your commandments;
and also that we, being defended from the fear of our enemies,
may live in peace and quietness;
through Jesus Christ our Savior,
who lives and reigns with you and the Holy Spirit, God forever.
Amen.

LORD'S PRAYER

Gathered into one by the Holy Spirit, let us pray as Jesus taught us:

A

**Our Father in heaven,
 hallowed be your name,
 your kingdom come,
 your will be done,
  on earth as in heaven.
Give us today our daily bread.
Forgive us our sins
 as we forgive those
  who sin against us.
Save us from the time of trial
 and deliver us from evil.
For the kingdom, the power,
 and the glory are yours,
  now and forever. Amen.**

B

**Our Father, who art in heaven,
 hallowed be thy name,
 thy kingdom come,
 thy will be done,
  on earth as it is in heaven.
Give us this day our daily bread;
and forgive us our trespasses,
 as we forgive those
  who trespass against us;
and lead us not into temptation,
 but deliver us from evil.
For thine is the kingdom,
 and the power, and the glory,
  forever and ever. Amen.**

BLESSING

Let us bless the Lord.
Thanks be to God.

A

The peace of God,
which surpasses all understanding,
guard our hearts and our minds in Christ Jesus.
Amen.

B

Almighty and merciful God,
the Father, the ☩ Son, and the Holy Spirit,
bless and preserve us.
Amen.

The greeting of peace may be shared by all. A hymn may be sung.

MORNING PRAYER *Matins*

OPENING

DIALOG

The leaders and the assembly may gather at the font. Morning prayer may begin with a dialog. The alleluia is omitted during Lent.

A
O Lord, open my lips,
and my mouth shall proclaim your praise.

**Glory to the Father, and to the Son,
and to the Holy Spirit:
as it was in the beginning, is now,
and will be forever. Amen. [Alleluia.]**

B
Satisfy us in the morning
with your steadfast love, O God,
**that we may rejoice
and be glad all our days.**

**Praise to the holy, life-giving,
and undivided Trinity:
always, now and ever,
and to the ages of ages. Amen. [Alleluia.]**

If the remembrance of baptism is omitted here, the liturgy continues with the psalmody on p. 13.

REMEMBRANCE OF BAPTISM

Especially on Sundays, morning prayer may include a remembrance of baptism, either here or at the conclusion of the liturgy. Water may be poured into the font.

The leader and the assembly give thanks for the gift of water and the grace of baptism.
The Lord be with you.
And also with you.

Let us give thanks to the Lord our God.
It is right to give our thanks and praise.

Ever-living God, author of creation,
we give you thanks for your gift of water
that brings life and refreshes the earth.
We bless and praise you, for by water and the Word
we are cleansed from sin and receive everlasting life.
Join us again this day to the saving death of Christ,
renew in us the living fountain of your grace,
and raise us with Christ Jesus to live in newness of life.

Honor and praise to you, merciful God,
for you love your whole creation,
and with all your creatures we give you glory,
through your Son Jesus Christ,
in the unity of the Holy Spirit, now and forever.
Amen.

Water from the font may be sprinkled over the people or they may be invited to use it to sign themselves with the cross. During this time a hymn, song, or canticle related to baptism may be sung.

At the conclusion of the remembrance, the leader addresses the assembly in these or similar words:
Almighty God,
who has given us a new birth
by water and the Holy Spirit,
and bestowed on us the forgiveness of sins,
keep us in eternal life
through the grace of Jesus Christ our Lord.
Amen.

PSALM AND SONG

PSALM R417–R420 ▶

The psalmody begins with Psalm 95:1-7a, Psalm 63, Psalm 100, or another psalm appropriate for morning. The psalm may be preceded and followed by the following or a seasonal antiphon.

A p. 26 ▶
Give glory to God, our light and our life.
Oh, come, let us worship and praise.

A time of silence follows. A psalm prayer may conclude the silence.

The psalmody may continue with one or more additional psalms. Each is followed by a time of silence, which may be concluded by a psalm prayer.

SONG

Additional assembly song may follow the psalmody, such as a hymn appropriate to the time of day or the season.

WORD

READINGS

One or more readings from scripture are proclaimed. Each reading may be concluded:

A	B
Holy wisdom, holy word.	The word of the Lord.
Thanks be to God.	**Thanks be to God.**

REFLECTION

The reading of scripture is followed by silence for reflection and meditation. Other forms of reflection may also follow, such as brief commentary, teaching, or personal witness; non-biblical readings; interpretation through music or other art forms; or guided conversation among those present.

The reflection may conclude with these or similar words:

A
The word is near you,
on your lips and in your heart.
**Everyone who calls on the name
of the Lord shall be saved.**

B
You have been born anew
through the living and abiding word of God.

GOSPEL CANTICLE

R421–R424 ▶

The gospel canticle for morning is the song of Zechariah (the Benedictus):

**Blessed are you, Lord, the God of Israel;
you have come to your people and set them free.
You have raised up for us a mighty Savior,
born of the house of your servant David.
Through your holy prophets, you promised of old
    to save us from our enemies,
    from the hands of all who hate us,
    to show mercy to our forebears,
    and to remember your holy covenant.
This was the oath you swore to our father Abraham:
    to set us free from the hands of our enemies,
    free to worship you without fear,
    holy and righteous before you,
    all the days of our life.**

**And you, child, shall be called the prophet of the Most High,
for you will go before the Lord to prepare the way,
to give God's people knowledge of salvation
by the forgiveness of their sins.
In the tender compassion of our God
the dawn from on high shall break upon us,
to shine on those who dwell in darkness and the shadow of death,
and to guide our feet into the way of peace.**

"We praise you, O God" (the Te Deum) may be used in place of the Benedictus (especially on festival days).   R425–R426 ▸

**We praise you, O God,
we acclaim you as Lord;
all creation worships you,
the Father everlasting.
To you all angels, all the powers of heaven,
the cherubim and seraphim, sing in endless praise:**
  **Holy, holy, holy Lord, God of power and might,
  heaven and earth are full of your glory.**
**The glorious company of apostles praise you.
The noble fellowship of prophets praise you.
The white-robed army of martyrs praise you.
Throughout the world the holy church acclaims you:**
  **Father, of majesty unbounded;
  your true and only Son, worthy of all praise;
  the Holy Spirit, advocate and guide.**

**You, Christ, are the king of glory,
the eternal Son of the Father.
When you took our flesh to set us free
you humbly chose the Virgin's womb.
You overcame the sting of death
and opened the kingdom of heaven to all believers.
You are seated at God's right hand in glory.
We believe that you will come to be our judge.**
  **Come, then, Lord, and help your people,
  bought with the price of your own blood,
  and bring us with your saints
  to glory everlasting.**

PRAYING

The leader and the assembly join in prayers of intercession and thanksgiving. The prayer of the day or the prayer of the previous Sunday may be said, followed by other collects or by another form of the prayers. The prayers conclude with the Lord's Prayer.

PRAYER OF THE DAY

The Lord be with you.
And also with you.

Let us pray.
At the conclusion of the prayer:
Amen.

Other prayers may be said, concluding with **Amen.**   p. 26 ▸

CONCLUDING PRAYER

A

Almighty and everlasting God,
you have brought us in safety to this new day.
Preserve us with your mighty power,
that we may not fall into sin,
nor be overcome in adversity.
In all we do, direct us to the fulfilling of your purpose;
through Jesus Christ our Lord.
Amen.

B

We give thanks to you, heavenly Father,
through Jesus Christ your dear Son,
that you have protected us through the night
from all danger and harm.
We ask you to preserve and keep us, this day also,
from all sin and evil,
that in all our thoughts, words, and deeds,
we may serve and please you.
Into your hands we commend
our bodies and souls and all that is ours.
Let your holy angels have charge of us,
that the wicked one have no power over us.
Amen.

C

O God,
you have called your servants to ventures
of which we cannot see the ending,
by paths as yet untrodden,
through perils unknown.
Give us faith to go out with good courage,
not knowing where we go,
but only that your hand is leading us
and your love supporting us;
through Jesus Christ our Lord.
Amen.

LORD'S PRAYER

Gathered into one by the Holy Spirit, let us pray as Jesus taught us:

A	B
Our Father in heaven, 　　**hallowed be your name,** 　　**your kingdom come,** 　　**your will be done,** 　　　　**on earth as in heaven.** **Give us today our daily bread.** **Forgive us our sins** 　　**as we forgive those** 　　　　**who sin against us.** **Save us from the time of trial** 　　**and deliver us from evil.** **For the kingdom, the power,** 　　**and the glory are yours,** 　　**now and forever. Amen.**	**Our Father, who art in heaven,** 　　**hallowed be thy name,** 　　**thy kingdom come,** 　　**thy will be done,** 　　　　**on earth as it is in heaven.** **Give us this day our daily bread;** **and forgive us our trespasses,** 　　**as we forgive those** 　　　　**who trespass against us;** **and lead us not into temptation,** 　　**but deliver us from evil.** **For thine is the kingdom,** 　　**and the power, and the glory,** 　　**forever and ever. Amen.**

If a remembrance of baptism (pp. 12–13) takes place here, the ministers move to the font for the remembrance of baptism. A hymn, song, or canticle related to baptism may be sung. The blessing that concludes the remembrance of baptism then serves as the final blessing of the liturgy.

BLESSING

Let us bless the Lord.
Thanks be to God.

Almighty and merciful God,
the Father, the ☩ Son, and the Holy Spirit,
bless and preserve us.
Amen.

The greeting of peace may be shared by all. A hymn may be sung.

NIGHT PRAYER *Compline*

OPENING

DIALOG

Night prayer may begin with a dialog between leader and assembly:
Almighty God grant us a quiet night
and peace at the last. Amen.

A	B
It is good to give thanks to the Lord,	By day, O God,
to sing praise to your name, O Most High;	**you grant your steadfast love,**
to herald your love in the morning,	and at night your song is with me,
your truth at the close of the day.	**a prayer to the God of my life.**

If the night hymn and confession are omitted, the liturgy continues with the psalmody on p. 19.

NIGHT HYMN

"All praise to thee, my God, this night" or another hymn appropriate to a night service may be sung.

CONFESSION

Let us confess our sin in the presence of God and of one another.

Silence for self-examination.

A
Holy and gracious God,
I confess that I have sinned against you this day.
Some of my sin I know—
the thoughts and words and deeds of which I am ashamed—
but some is known only to you.
In the name of Jesus Christ I ask forgiveness.
Deliver and restore me, that I may rest in peace.

By the mercy of God we are united with Jesus Christ,
in whom we are forgiven.
We rest now in the peace of Christ
and rise in the morning to serve.

B
I confess to God Almighty,
before the whole company of heaven,
and to you, my brothers and sisters,
that I have sinned by my own fault
in thought, word, and deed.
I pray God Almighty to have mercy on me,
forgive me all my sins,
and bring me to everlasting life.
Almighty and merciful God
grant you pardon, forgiveness, and remission of all your sins.

I confess to God Almighty,
before the whole company of heaven,
and to you, my brothers and sisters,
that I have sinned by my own fault
in thought, word, and deed.
I pray God Almighty to have mercy on me,
forgive me all my sins,
and bring me to everlasting life.
Almighty and merciful God
grant you pardon, forgiveness, and remission of all your sins.

The greeting of peace may be shared by all.

PSALM AND SONG

PSALM

One or more psalms (such as 4, 33, 34, 91, 130, 134, 136) are sung or said. Each is followed by a time of silence, which may be concluded by a psalm prayer.

SONG

A hymn or song appropriate to the time of day or the season may be sung.

WORD

READING

A brief scripture reading is proclaimed.

A

Hear, O Israel: The Lord is our God, the Lord alone. You shall love the Lord your God with all your heart, and with all your soul, and with all your might. Keep these words that I am commanding you today in your heart. Recite them to your children and talk about them when you are at home and when you are away, when you lie down and when you rise. (Deuteronomy 6:4-7)

B

You, O Lord, are in the midst of us, and we are called by your name; do not forsake us, O Lord our God.   (Jeremiah 14:9)

C

Do not worry, saying, "What will we eat?" or "What will we drink?" or "What will we wear?" Indeed your heavenly Father knows that you need all these things. But strive first for the dominion and the righteousness of God, and all these things will be given to you as well. So do not worry about tomorrow.   (Matthew 6:31, 32b-34a)

D

Come to me, all you that are weary and are carrying heavy burdens, and I will give you rest. Take my yoke upon you, and learn from me; for I am gentle and humble in heart, and you will find rest for your souls. For my yoke is easy, and my burden is light. (Matthew 11:28-30)

E

Peace is my parting gift to you, my own peace, such as the world cannot give. Set your troubled hearts at rest, and banish your fears.   (John 14:27)

F

I am convinced that neither death, nor life, nor angels, nor rulers, nor things present, nor things to come, nor powers, nor height, nor depth, nor anything else in all creation, will be able to separate us from the love of God in Christ Jesus our Lord.   (Romans 8:38-39)

G

It is the God who said, "Let light shine out of darkness," who has shone in our hearts to give the light of the knowledge of the glory of God in the face of Jesus Christ. But we have this treasure in clay jars, so that it may be made clear that this extraordinary power belongs to God and does not come from us. We are afflicted in every way, but not crushed; perplexed, but not driven to despair; persecuted, but not forsaken; struck down, but not destroyed; always carrying in the body the death of Jesus, so that the life of Jesus may also be made be visible in our bodies.   (2 Corinthians 4:6-10)

H

Humble yourselves under God's mighty hand, so that God may exalt you in due time. Cast all your anxiety on the one who cares for you. Discipline yourselves, keep alert. Like a roaring lion, your adversary the devil prowls around, looking for someone to devour. Resist the devil, steadfast in your faith.   (1 Peter 5:6-9a)

I

There will be no more night; the servants of God need no light of lamp or sun, for the Lord God will be their light, and they will reign forever and ever.   (Revelation 22:5)

REFLECTION

The reading of scripture is followed by silence for reflection and meditation. The silence may conclude with a responsory:

A
Into your hands I commend my spirit.
Into your hands I commend my spirit.

You have redeemed me, faithful God.
Into your hands I commend my spirit.

Glory to the Father, and to the Son,
and to the Holy Spirit.
Into your hands I commend my spirit.

B
You have redeemed me, faithful God.
Into your hands I commend my spirit.

GOSPEL CANTICLE

The gospel canticle for night prayer is the song of Simeon (the Nunc dimittis). As an alternative, the canticle may be sung after the Lord's Prayer and before the concluding blessing.

Guide us waking, O Lord, and guard us sleeping;
that awake we may watch with Christ
and asleep we may rest in peace.

Now, Lord, you let your servant go in peace:
your word has been fulfilled.
My own eyes have seen the salvation
which you have prepared in the sight of every people:
a light to reveal you to the nations
and the glory of your people Israel.

Guide us waking, O Lord, and guard us sleeping;
that awake we may watch with Christ
and asleep we may rest in peace.

PRAYING

The prayers follow. One or more of the following prayers or another form of the prayers may be used. The prayers conclude with the Lord's Prayer.

PRAYERS

Hear my prayer, O Lord;
listen to my cry.

Keep me as the apple of your eye;
hide me under the shadow of your wings.

In righteousness I shall see you;
when I awake, your presence will give me joy.

A

Be present, merciful God,
and protect us through the hours of this night,
so that we who are wearied by the changes and chances of life
may find our rest in you;
through Jesus Christ our Lord.
Amen.

B

O Lord, support us all the day long of this troubled life,
until the shadows lengthen and the evening comes
and the busy world is hushed,
the fever of life is over, and our work is done.
Then, in your mercy, grant us a safe lodging,
and a holy rest, and peace at the last;
through Jesus Christ our Lord.
Amen.

C

Be our light in the darkness, O God,
and in your great mercy defend us
from all perils and dangers of this night;
for the love of your only Son, our Savior Jesus Christ.
Amen.

D

Keep watch, dear Lord,
with those who work or watch or weep this night,
and give your angels charge over those who sleep.
Tend the sick, give rest to the weary, bless the dying,
soothe the suffering, comfort the afflicted, shield the joyous;
and all for your love's sake.
Amen.

E

Eternal God,
the hours both of day and night are yours,
and to you the darkness is no threat.
Be present, we pray, with those who labor in these hours of night,
especially those who watch and work on behalf of others.
Grant them diligence in their watching, faithfulness in their service,
courage in danger, and competence in emergencies.
Help them to meet the needs of others with confidence and compassion;
through Jesus Christ our Lord.
Amen.

F

Gracious God, we give you thanks for the day,
especially for the good we were permitted to give and to receive;
the day is now past and we commit it to you.
We entrust to you the night; we rest securely,
for you are our help, and you neither slumber nor sleep;
through Jesus Christ our Lord.
Amen.

LORD'S PRAYER

Gathered into one by the Holy Spirit, let us pray as Jesus taught us:

A

**Our Father in heaven,
  hallowed be your name,
  your kingdom come,
  your will be done,
    on earth as in heaven.
Give us today our daily bread.
Forgive us our sins
  as we forgive those
    who sin against us.
Save us from the time of trial
  and deliver us from evil.
For the kingdom, the power,
  and the glory are yours,
  now and forever. Amen.**

B

**Our Father, who art in heaven,
  hallowed be thy name,
  thy kingdom come,
  thy will be done,
    on earth as it is in heaven.
Give us this day our daily bread;
and forgive us our trespasses,
  as we forgive those
    who trespass against us;
and lead us not into temptation,
  but deliver us from evil.
For thine is the kingdom,
  and the power, and the glory,
  forever and ever. Amen.**

BLESSING

A

Let us bless the Lord.
Thanks be to God.

Almighty and merciful God,
Father, ☩ Son, and Holy Spirit,
bless, preserve, and keep us,
this night and forevermore.
Amen.

B

Now in peace I will lie down and sleep;
you alone, O God, make me secure.

Let us bless the Lord.
Thanks be to God.

Supplemental Materials

EVENING PRAYER

DIALOG

C
Light and peace in Jesus Christ our Lord.
Thanks be to God.

D (Advent)
The Spirit and the church cry out:
Come, Lord Jesus.

All those who await his appearance pray:
Come, Lord Jesus.

The whole creation pleads:
Come, Lord Jesus.

E (Christmas, Epiphany of Our Lord, and Baptism of Our Lord)
The light shines in the darkness,
and the darkness has not overcome it.

The Word became flesh and lived among us,
and we have beheld Christ's glory.

To us a child is born, to us a Son is given.
In the Word was life, and the life was the light of all people.

F (Lent)
Behold, now is the acceptable time;
now is the day of salvation.

Turn us again, O God of our salvation,
that the light of your face may shine on us.

May your justice shine like the sun;
and may the poor be lifted up.

G (Easter)
Jesus Christ is risen from the dead.
Alleluia, alleluia, alleluia!

We are illumined by the brightness of his rising.
Alleluia, alleluia, alleluia!

Death has no more dominion over us.
Alleluia, alleluia, alleluia!

THANKSGIVING FOR LIGHT

B
We praise and thank you, O God,
for you are without beginning and without end.
You made the day for the works of light
and the night for the refreshment of creation.
Loving Lord, source of all that is good,
mercifully receive our evening praise and thanksgiving.
As you have led us through the day
and brought us to night's beginning,
keep us now in Christ;
grant us a peaceful evening and a night free from sin;
and, at the end, bring us to everlasting life in Christ our Lord,
through whom we offer glory, honor, and worship
to you in the Holy Spirit,
now and always and forever and ever.
Amen.

C
We give you thanks and praise, O God,
for your Son Jesus, the Light of the world.
In the beginning your creation was filled with radiance;
your energy brought into being
galaxies, stars, planets, and every living thing.
By the gift of light you give life
to all that grows on earth and sustains our lives.
By the light of your wisdom
we come to know and rejoice in your vast creation.
Through this day you have illumined our path.
Now, as night falls,
we praise you for the splendor of the heavens,
and we look to the true radiance, Jesus Christ our Lord,
through whom we give glory and honor
to you in the Holy Spirit, now and forever.
Amen.

MORNING PRAYER

PSALM ANTIPHON

B (Advent)
Blessed is the one who comes in the name of the Lord.
Oh, come, let us worship and praise.

C (Christmas, Epiphany of Our Lord, and Baptism of Our Lord)
I bring you good news of a great joy:
to you is born a Savior, Christ the Lord.
Oh, come, let us worship and praise.

D (Lent)
The Sun of righteousness will arise
with healing in his wings.
Oh, come, let us worship and praise.

E (Easter)
Alleluia. Christ is risen indeed.
Oh, come, let us worship and praise.

PRAYERS

Prayers using the following pattern may follow the prayer of the day. A brief silence follows each thanksgiving and intercession.

Mighty God of mercy, we thank you for the resurrection dawn bringing the glory of our risen Lord who makes every day new. Especially we thank you for
    the beauty of your creation . . .
    the new creation in Christ and all gifts of healing and forgiveness . . .
    the sustaining love of family and friends . . .
    the communion of faith in your church . . .
        Other thanksgivings may be added.

Merciful God of might, renew this weary world, heal the hurts of all your children, and bring about your peace for all in Christ Jesus, the living Lord. Especially we pray for
    those who govern nations of the world . . .
    the people in countries ravaged by strife or warfare . . .
    all who work for peace and international harmony . . .
    all who strive to save the earth from destruction . . .
    the church of Jesus Christ in every land . . .
        Other intercessions may be added.
        A concluding prayer and the Lord's Prayer (pp. 16–17) complete the prayers.

REMEMBRANCE OF BAPTISM

Paschal Blessing

Especially on Sundays, the paschal blessing may be used as the remembrance of baptism at the conclusion of morning prayer. A hymn related to baptism may be sung as the ministers (and the assembly) come to the font.

As many as have been baptized into Christ have put on Christ.
Alleluia.

On the first day of the week at early dawn, the women came to the tomb, taking the spices that they had prepared. They found the stone rolled away from the tomb, but when they went in they did not find the body. While they were perplexed about this, suddenly two men in dazzling clothes stood beside them. The women were terrified and bowed their faces to the ground, but the men said to them: "Why do you look for the living among the dead? Remember how he told you, while he was still in Galilee, that the Son of man must be handed over to sinners, and be crucified, and on the third day rise."

The Te Deum is sung. R425–R426 ▶

Water from the font may be sprinkled over the people during the singing of the canticle.

O God,
for our redemption you gave your only Son to suffer death on the cross,
and by his glorious resurrection you delivered us from the power of death.
Make us die every day to sin so that we may rise to live with Christ forever;
who lives and reigns with you and the Holy Spirit, one God, now and forever.
Amen.

Almighty God bless us, and direct our days and our deeds in peace.
Amen.

DAILY PRAYER
Pattern and Examples for Personal and Small Group Prayer

Many people find that the church's liturgies for common daily prayer serve them well when they are praying alone or with others in the household or other small groups. They are able to set aside particular times for regular prayer and to use or adapt the materials for evening, morning, and/or the close of day. For many other people, however, the demands of work, school, and household life make it difficult or impossible to pray or meditate at a regular time each day. The simplest forms of prayer may be their daily companions: a whispered plea for help, a word of thanksgiving, the repetition of a brief phrase of scripture or song, a prayerful speaking of God's names, the Lord's Prayer, brief prayers at table, bedtime prayers with children.

Even in the midst of busy lives, however, people are often looking for a more intentional and focused approach to prayer. In a world where the values and priorities of everyday life often compete with the ways of God, how can Christians be open to the workings of the Holy Spirit in their daily lives? How can they see their various vocations as God's calling to them and their daily activity as God's work in the world? How can they move beyond isolation in their own thoughts, needs, and wants to embrace the needs of others and identify themselves with Christ's mission?

The church's foundational pattern for daily prayer offers a natural way of praying that is highly adaptable to a variety of contexts and personal situations. That pattern, described in the Shape of the Rite for Daily Prayer in Common (pp. 3–5), is described in another way in the narrative that follows, for use in personal prayer or when praying with others in a small group. It is important to see such an approach to daily prayer as not merely an abridgement or truncating of the assembly liturgies; the pattern has its own integrity and may be realized in a variety of circumstances.

Following this narrative description of a pattern for personal and small group prayer, several examples for prayer in small groups are outlined. These examples are just a few illustrations of the possibilities for such gatherings for prayer and are not intended to present a normative practice.

OPENING

Beginning to pray often involves simply setting apart time and a place to pray—a comfortable chair by a window, a table with a lighted candle, a car or bus on the daily commute, an outdoor bench, a conference room at work, a Sunday school room for a committee meeting. Dedicated space and time bring focus and help to center the heart and mind. Beginning to pray is an opening of the self to God, and yet this opening is not merely one's own spiritual exercise: the Spirit of God opens our hearts, and the Spirit intercedes even when our words fail (Rom. 8:26).

PSALM, SONG, WORD

"Be still, and know that I am God" (Ps. 46:10). Much of prayer is, in fact, listening in quiet for God's voice. The word of God—read, reflected upon, responded to—is the primary avenue for this listening. The psalms provide a particular gift to daily praying. Many of them are highly personal expressions of the whole range of human experience. They serve both as God's word to us and, on our lips, our response to God in praise, plea, lament, thanksgiving. It may be just the refrain from the Sunday psalm that carries one through the week, or one may follow a course of reading through the whole psalter. Scripture verses from the Sunday assembly, from one of the patterns for daily Bible reading, or selected to address a particular need in one's life or a group's work, further engage the word of God. The witness of the scriptures may be amplified through readings, poetry, and songs from God's faithful people throughout the centuries, including present-day witnesses to the faith. Silent time for reflection, alone or in a group, enables further listening for God's voice. Speaking to one another in reflection upon God's word is an expression of the "mutual conversation and consolation" of Christian sisters and brothers identified by the Lutheran confessions as one of the marks of the church.

PRAYING

Listening to the voice of God leads to praying. This praying is shaped by that word of God and by the needs and circumstances of life. Praying not only for our own needs but the needs of others, for healing, for justice, for our enemies, for well-being, for peace, for the sick and the dying, and for the reign of God are some of the ways that our response to God's power in our lives can be expressed. This time of praying may be gathered up in the Lord's Prayer. This prayer, always prayed when Christians gather at the holy meal, links us to the worship of the whole church: we pray with Christ to our Father and are gathered with all other Christians through the working of the Holy Spirit. This time of praying may be punctuated with a brief word of blessing or commendation that sends us back into the rhythm of daily life, where our various callings lead us in many directions to carry on God's work in the world.

Morning Prayer
An Example for Use by a Group before the Day's Activity

This example is intended to give one illustration of how the pattern for daily prayer might be realized to meet the needs of a particular context, and is not intended to present a normative use.

OPENING

After gathering and greeting one another in your group, you may keep a brief silence.

A
The steadfast love of the Lord never ceases,
God's mercies never come to an end;
they are new every morning;
great is your faithfulness.

B
We await the blessings of this day.
Come, Lord Jesus.
We open ourselves to God's word.
Come, Lord Jesus.
We offer ourselves for prayer and service.
Come, Lord Jesus.

PSALM, SONG

A psalm, or a portion of a psalm, may be read by one person or by the group. You may use a psalm especially appropriate for morning (such as 95:1-7a; 63; 100) or a psalm related to the Sunday readings.

A hymn, a brief memorized refrain, or another song may be sung or spoken.

WORD

The reading may be one of the Sunday readings or a portion thereof, or a reading from a daily lectionary, or another selected scripture reading.

After a time of silence for reflection and meditation, members of the group may offer some of their reflections especially as to how this passage relates to their daily work or other activity.

This response may conclude the time of reflection:
You have been born anew
through the living and abiding word of God.

PRAYING

You may take some time to talk about the joys, concerns, needs, and hopes each person brings this morning. One or more from the group may gather these and speak prayers, or any who wish may be invited to offer prayers.

Close with Luther's Morning Prayer and the Lord's Prayer.

We give thanks to you, heavenly Father,
through Jesus Christ your dear Son,
that you have protected us through the night
from all danger and harm.
We ask you to preserve and keep us, this day also,
from all sin and evil,
that in all our thoughts, words, and deeds,
we may serve and please you.
Into your hands we commend
our bodies and souls and all that is ours.
Let your holy angels have charge of us,
that the wicked one have no power over us.
Amen.

A
Our Father in heaven,
 hallowed be your name,
 your kingdom come,
 your will be done,
  on earth as in heaven.
Give us today our daily bread.
Forgive us our sins
 as we forgive those
  who sin against us.
Save us from the time of trial
 and deliver us from evil.
For the kingdom, the power,
 and the glory are yours,
 now and forever. Amen.

B
Our Father, who art in heaven,
 hallowed be thy name,
 thy kingdom come,
 thy will be done,
  on earth as it is in heaven.
Give us this day our daily bread;
and forgive us our trespasses,
 as we forgive those
  who trespass against us;
and lead us not into temptation,
 but deliver us from evil.
For thine is the kingdom,
 and the power, and the glory,
 forever and ever. Amen.

Let us bless the Lord.
Thanks be to God.

You may exchange a sign and word of peace.

Evening Prayer
An Example for Opening a Congregation Council Meeting

This example is intended to give one illustration of how the pattern for daily prayer might be realized to meet the needs of a particular context, and is not intended to present a normative use.

OPENING

The leader may light a candle and place it in front of or in the center of the group, while saying:
We belong to Christ,
in whom we have been baptized.

Keep a time of silence.

From the joys and satisfactions, the cares and concerns of our lives,
gather us in, O God.
For attention to your presence, for thanksgiving and praise,
gather us in, O God.
For comfort and solace, for encouragement and strength,
gather us in, O God.
For this community and for this time of prayer,
gather us in, O God.

PSALM, SONG

A psalm, or a portion of a psalm, may be read by one person or by the group. You may use a psalm especially appropriate for evening (such as 141, 121, 134) or a psalm related to the Sunday readings.

A hymn, a brief memorized refrain, or another song may be sung or spoken.

WORD

The reading may be one of the Sunday readings or a portion thereof, or a reading from a daily lectionary, or another selected scripture reading.

After a time of silence for reflection and meditation, one or more members of the group may offer some of their reflections especially as to how this passage relates to their lives or to the work of the council.

This response may conclude the time of reflection:
Your word, O God, is a lamp to my feet,
and a light to my path.

PRAYING

Let us give thanks for God's blessings to us especially today.
Here blessings may be named silently or aloud.
God of love,
hear our prayer.

Let us bring before God needs and concerns known to us.
Here people and situations, especially in the congregation, may be named silently or aloud.
God of love,
hear our prayer.

Let us bring before God our own needs.
Here specific needs may be mentioned silently or aloud.
God of love,
hear our prayer.

Let us ask for God's guidance and blessing upon our meeting this evening.
Here specific items before the council may be mentioned silently or aloud.
God of love,
hear our prayer.

A

**Our Father in heaven,
   hallowed be your name,
   your kingdom come,
   your will be done,
     on earth as in heaven.
Give us today our daily bread.
Forgive us our sins
   as we forgive those
     who sin against us.
Save us from the time of trial
   and deliver us from evil.
For the kingdom, the power,
   and the glory are yours,
     now and forever. Amen.**

B

**Our Father, who art in heaven,
   hallowed be thy name,
   thy kingdom come,
   thy will be done,
     on earth as it is in heaven.
Give us this day our daily bread;
and forgive us our trespasses,
   as we forgive those
     who trespass against us;
and lead us not into temptation,
   but deliver us from evil.
For thine is the kingdom,
   and the power, and the glory,
     forever and ever. Amen.**

May God bless us and bless the work we are called to do in Jesus' name.
Amen.

Night Prayer
An Example for Use in the Household

This example is intended to give one illustration of how the pattern for daily prayer might be realized to meet the needs of a particular context, and is not intended to present a normative use.

OPENING

The leader may light a candle and place it in the center of the group, while saying:
Remember the words of baptism.
We have been sealed with the Holy Spirit,
and marked with the ☩ cross of Christ forever.

You may keep a brief time of silence.

From the rising of the sun to its setting,
let God's name be praised.

You may take some time to remember and talk about the blessings of the day, or the times and places where you have been aware of God's presence and the working of the Holy Spirit.

Create in me a clean heart, O God,
and renew a right spirit within me.

You may take some time to remember and talk about those times and places where you have wandered from your baptismal identity, when you have knowingly or unknowingly sinned against God or another person.

By the mercy of God we are united with Jesus Christ,
in whom we are forgiven.
**We rest now in the peace of Christ
and rise in the morning to serve.**

You may exchange a sign and word of peace.

WORD

One of those present may read a psalm or another brief scripture reading. You may reflect on the reading silently and aloud.

This response may conclude the time of reflection:
You have redeemed me, faithful God.
Into your hands I commend my spirit.

PRAYING

Gracious God, we give you thanks for the day,
especially for the good we were permitted to give and to receive;
the day is now past and we commit it to you.
We entrust to you the night;
we rest securely, for you are our help,
and you neither slumber nor sleep.
Amen.

Members of the household may offer particular prayers of thanksgiving or intercession, especially those related to earlier conversation.

A

**Our Father in heaven,
   hallowed be your name,
   your kingdom come,
   your will be done,
     on earth as in heaven.
Give us today our daily bread.
Forgive us our sins
   as we forgive those
     who sin against us.
Save us from the time of trial
   and deliver us from evil.
For the kingdom, the power,
   and the glory are yours,
     now and forever. Amen.**

B

**Our Father, who art in heaven,
   hallowed be thy name,
   thy kingdom come,
   thy will be done,
     on earth as it is in heaven.
Give us this day our daily bread;
and forgive us our trespasses,
   as we forgive those
     who trespass against us;
and lead us not into temptation,
   but deliver us from evil.
For thine is the kingdom,
   and the power, and the glory,
     forever and ever. Amen.**

Guide us waking, O Lord, and guard us sleeping;
**that awake we may watch with Christ,
and asleep we may rest in peace.**

Almighty and merciful God, Father, ☩ Son, and Holy Spirit,
bless, preserve, and keep us, this night and forevermore.
Amen.

Prayer of Lament
An Example of Daily Prayer in a Time of Need

This example is intended to give one illustration of how the pattern for daily prayer might be realized to meet the needs of a particular context and circumstance, and is not intended to present a normative use. In this example, the elements of psalm/song/word and praying unfold within each of the movements of lament, petition, and thanksgiving. 'Ad 'anah 'Adonai (hahd ah-nah ah-doh-nye) is Hebrew for "How long, O Lord?"

OPENING

O God, be not far from us.
Come quickly to help us, O God.

The Lord is near to those who call.
Oh, come, let us worship the Lord.

LAMENT

PSALM 13

'Ad 'anah 'Adonai, how long?
'Ad 'anah 'Adonai, how long?

How long, O Lord?
Will you forget me forever?
How long will you hide your face from me?
How long will I wrestle within myself?
Will sorrow be within my heart day after day?
How long will my enemy triumph over me?

'Ad 'anah 'Adonai, how long?
'Ad 'anah 'Adonai, how long?

PRAYING

Prayers of lamentation are spoken on behalf of the world, the society, and the local community.

Silence for reflection and meditation follows. A musical response may also follow.

All speak the concluding prayer:
O Lord, we are in great need. How long will you forget us?
Our life is difficult, and yet you hide your face from us.
We are troubled; day after day our problems remain; we find no help.
How long, O Lord, will our enemies triumph over us?

PETITION

PSALM 13

'Ad 'anah 'Adonai, how long?
'Ad 'anah 'Adonai, how long?

Look at me; answer me, O Lord my God.
Enlighten my eyes lest I sleep the sleep of death,
lest my enemy says, "I have defeated you";
lest my adversaries rejoice because I am shaken.

'Ad 'anah 'Adonai, how long?
'Ad 'anah 'Adonai, how long?

PRAYING

Petitions and intercessions are spoken on behalf of the world, the society, and the local community.

Silence for reflection and meditation follows. A musical response may also follow.

All speak the concluding prayer:
O Lord, look upon us and answer us!
Lead us through the time of trial.
Grant us light to see the way.
Let us not be defeated, lest we become the delight of our enemies.

THANKSGIVING

PSALM 13

'Ad 'anah 'Adonai, how long?
'Ad 'anah 'Adonai, how long?

But I trust in your unfailing love;
my heart rejoices in your salvation.
Let me sing to the Lord,
who has dealt bountifully with me.

'Ad 'anah 'Adonai, how long?
'Ad 'anah 'Adonai, how long?

PRAYING

Prayers of thanksgiving are spoken on behalf of the world, the society, and the local community.

Silence for reflection and meditation follows. A musical response may also follow.

All speak the concluding prayer:
O Lord, we trust in your unfailing love.
Our hearts rejoice in your salvation,
for you are near to those who call upon you.
We sing praise to you for your most bounteous gift,
Jesus Christ, your Son, our Lord. Amen.

Almighty God bless us,
guide us and defend us,
and lead us into life.
Amen.

Psalms
for Daily Prayer

PSALMS for DAILY PRAYER
Examples of Approaches to Psalm Translation

Psalm translation is an important issue to consider in the preparation of new worship materials, because the psalms are used frequently in many facets of the church's worship life. The use of the psalms is especially central to the church's liturgies of daily prayer; thus this section of examples of approaches to psalm translation is included with this daily prayer provisional resource.

The questions about psalm translation include these. Is there a single, consistent translation used throughout a family of worship resources—or might there be multiple approaches to translation? Do translations used in worship correlate to translations commonly used in Bible reading and study—or are there translations that are distinctive to their use in worship (as is the case, for example, with the words of institution and the Lord's Prayer)? To what extent do translations for use in worship attend to the principle that "the language of worship embraces all" (*Principles for Worship,* L-15)? How important is the factor of ecumenical usage?

The following selection of psalms presents three approaches to psalm translation for liturgical use. Included in this selection are psalms that are frequently associated with daily prayer. Additional psalms that are part of the Sunday lectionary, together with musical possibilities for singing the psalms, are presented on the Renewing Worship Web site, www.renewingworship.org.

The first approach to psalm translation presented here is that of the New Revised Standard Version of the Bible (NRSV). This is a widely-used ecumenical translation of the scriptures. It is designed as a close translation of the biblical text for study and public reading.

The second approach to psalm translation presented here is an emended version of the NRSV, prepared for the *New Century Hymnal.* This version follows the NRSV text, except that gender-specific language for human beings and God is consistently emended so that it is not gender-specific.

The third approach to psalm translation presented here is an emended version of the translation in *Lutheran Book of Worship,* which itself is drawn from *The Book of Common Prayer.* This version retains significant ties to the memory base of liturgical psalm use and attempts to preserve the original version's design for use in public prayer and singing. Some emendations represent an effort to make the version more closely reflect the Hebrew poetry. Gender-inclusive language for human beings is used consistently. Gender-specific language for God is generally avoided, although it may remain in psalms that rely on a gender-specific metaphor for God.

Feedback during the provisional period about the use of these or other approaches to psalm translation will be crucial as recommendations are made for the use of the psalms in longer-term resources.

PSALM 4
NRSV

¹ Answer me when I call,
 O God of my right!
You gave me room when I was in distress.
 Be gracious to me, and hear my prayer.
² How long, you people, shall my honor suffer shame?
 How long will you love vain words, and seek after lies?
³ But know that the Lord has set apart the faithful for himself;
 the Lord hears when I call to him.
⁴ When you are disturbed, do not sin;
 ponder it on your beds, and be silent.
⁵ Offer right sacrifices,
 and put your trust in the Lord.
⁶ There are many who say, "Oh, that we might see some good!
 Let the light of your face shine on us, O Lord!"
⁷ You have put gladness in my heart
 more than when their grain and wine abound.
⁸ I will both lie down and sleep in peace;
 for you alone, O Lord, make me lie down in safety.

PSALM 4
NRSV, emended

¹ Answer me when I call,
 O God of my right!
You gave me room when I was in distress.
 Be gracious to me, and hear my prayer.
² How long, you people, shall my honor suffer shame?
 How long will you love vain words, and seek after lies?
³ But know that God has set apart the faithful for God;
 God hears when I call.
⁴ When you are disturbed, do not sin;
 ponder it on your beds, and be silent.
⁵ Offer right sacrifices,
 and put your trust in God.
⁶ There are many who say, "Oh, that we might see some good!
 Let the light of your face shine on us, O God!"
⁷ You have put gladness in my heart
 more than when their grain and wine abound.
⁸ I will both lie down and sleep in peace;
 for you alone, O God, make me lie down in safety.

PSALM 4
LBW, emended

¹ Answer me when I call, O God, defender of my cause;
 you set me free when I am in distress;
 have mercy on me and hear my prayer.

² "You mortals, how long will you dishonor my glory;
>   how long will you love illusions and seek after lies?"
³ Know that the Lord does wonders for the faithful;
>   the Lord will hear me when I call.
⁴ Tremble, then, and do not sin;
>   speak to your heart in silence upon your bed.
⁵ Offer the appointed sacrifices,
>   and put your trust in the Lord.
⁶ Many are saying, "Who will show us any good!"
>   Let the light of your face shine upon us, O Lord.
⁷ You have put gladness in my heart
>   more than when grain and wine abound.
⁸ In peace, I will lie down and sleep;
>   for you alone, O Lord, make me rest secure.

PSALM 8
NRSV

¹ O Lord, our Sovereign, how majestic is your name in all the earth!
>   You have set your glory above the heavens.
² Out of the mouths of babes and infants you have founded a bulwark because of your foes,
>   to silence the enemy and the avenger.
³ When I look at your heavens, the work of your fingers,
>   the moon and the stars that you have established;
⁴ what are human beings that you are mindful of them,
>   mortals that you care for them?
⁵ Yet you have made them a little lower than God,
>   and crowned them with glory and honor.
⁶ You have given them dominion over the works of your hands;
>   you have put all things under their feet,
⁷ all sheep and oxen, and also the beasts of the field,
>   ⁸ the birds of the air, and the fish of the sea, whatever passes along the paths
>   of the seas.
⁹ O Lord, our Sovereign,
>   how majestic is your name in all the earth!

PSALM 8
NRSV, emended

¹ O God, our Sovereign, how majestic is your name in all the earth!
>   You have set your glory above the heavens.
² Out of the mouths of babes and infants you have founded a bulwark because of your foes,
>   to silence the enemy and the avenger.
³ When I look at your heavens, the work of your fingers,
>   the moon and the stars that you have established;
⁴ what are human beings that you are mindful of them,
>   mortals that you care for them?

⁵ Yet you have made them a little lower than God,
    and crowned them with glory and honor.
⁶ You have given them dominion over the works of your hands;
    you have put all things under their feet,
⁷ all sheep and oxen, and also the beasts of the field,
    ⁸ the birds of the air, and the fish of the sea, whatever passes along the paths of the seas.
⁹ O God, our Sovereign,
    how majestic is your name in all the earth!

PSALM 8
LBW, emended

¹ O LORD our Lord,
    how majestic is your name in all the earth!—
² you whose glory is chanted above the heavens
    out of the mouths of babes and infants.
You have set up a fortress against your enemies,
    to silence the foe and avenger.
³ When I look at your heavens, the work of your fingers,
    the moon and the stars you have set in their places,
⁴ what are mere mortals that you should be mindful of them,
    human beings that you should care for them?
⁵ Yet you have made them little less than divine;
    with glory and honor you crown them.
⁶ You have made them rule over the works of your hands;
    you have put all things under their feet:
⁷ all flocks and cattle,
    even the wild beasts of the field,
⁸ the birds of the air, the fish of the sea,
    and whatever passes along the paths of the sea.
⁹ O LORD our Lord,
    how majestic is your name in all the earth!

PSALM 23
NRSV

¹ The LORD is my shepherd, I shall not want.
    ² He makes me lie down in green pastures; he leads me beside still waters;
³ he restores my soul.
    He leads me in right paths for his name's sake.
⁴ Even though I walk through the darkest valley, I fear no evil;
    for you are with me; your rod and your staff—they comfort me.
⁵ You prepare a table before me in the presence of my enemies;
    you anoint my head with oil; my cup overflows.
⁶ Surely goodness and mercy shall follow me all the days of my life,
    and I shall dwell in the house of the LORD my whole life long.

PSALM 23
NRSV, emended

¹ God is my shepherd, I shall not want.
  ² God makes me lie down in green pastures, and leads me beside still waters;
³ God restores my soul,
  and leads me in right paths for the sake of God's name.
⁴ Even though I walk through the darkest valley, I fear no evil;
  for you are with me; your rod and your staff—they comfort me.
⁵ You prepare a table before me in the presence of my enemies;
  you anoint my head with oil; my cup overflows.
⁶ Surely goodness and mercy shall follow me all the days of my life,
  and I shall dwell in the house of God my whole life long.

PSALM 23
LBW, emended

¹ The LORD is my shepherd;
  I shall not be in want.
² You make me lie down in green pastures;
  beside serene waters you lead me.
³ You revive my spirit.
  You guide me in right paths to uphold your name.
⁴ Even when I walk through the valley of the shadow of death,
I will fear no evil;
  for you are with me; your rod and your staff, they comfort me.
⁵ You spread out a table before me in the presence of my enemies;
  you anoint my head with oil, and my cup overflows.
⁶ Surely goodness and mercy shall follow me all the days of my life,
  and I will dwell in the house of the LORD forever.

PSALM 24
NRSV

¹ The earth is the LORD's and all that is in it,
  the world, and those who live in it;
² for he has founded it on the seas,
  and established it on the rivers.
³ Who shall ascend the hill of the LORD?
  And who shall stand in his holy place?
⁴ Those who have clean hands and pure hearts,
  who do not lift up their souls to what is false, and do not swear deceitfully.
⁵ They will receive blessing from the LORD,
  and vindication from the God of their salvation.
⁶ Such is the company of those who seek him,
  who seek the face of the God of Jacob.
⁷ Lift up your heads, O gates! and be lifted up, O ancient doors!
  that the King of glory may come in.

⁸ Who is the King of glory?
    The Lord, strong and mighty, the Lord, mighty in battle.
⁹ Lift up your heads, O gates! and be lifted up, O ancient doors!
    that the King of glory may come in.
¹⁰ Who is this King of glory?
    The Lord of hosts, he is the King of glory.

PSALM 24
NRSV, emended

¹ The earth is God's and all that is in it,
    the world, and those who live in it;
² for God has founded it on the seas,
    and established it on the rivers.
³ Who shall ascend the hill of God?
    And who shall stand in God's holy place?
⁴ Those who have clean hands and pure hearts,
    who do not lift up their souls to what is false, and do not swear deceitfully.
⁵ They will receive blessing from God,
    and vindication from the God of their salvation.
⁶ Such is the company of those who seek God,
    who seek the face of the God of Jacob.
⁷ Lift up your heads, O gates! and be lifted up, O ancient doors!
    that the Ruler of glory may come in.
⁸ Who is the Ruler of glory?
    God, strong and mighty, God, mighty in battle.
⁹ Lift up your heads, O gates! and be lifted up, O ancient doors!
    that the Ruler of glory may come in.
¹⁰ Who is this Ruler of glory?
    The Sovereign of hosts—God is the Ruler of glory.

PSALM 24
LBW, emended

¹ The earth is the Lord's and all its fullness,
    the world and those who dwell therein.
² For the Lord has founded it upon the seas
    and established it upon the rivers of the deep.
³ Who may ascend the mountain of the Lord,
    and who may stand in God's holy place?
⁴ Those of innocent hands and purity of heart,
    who do not lift their souls to an idol, nor do they swear by what is false—
⁵ they shall receive blessing from the Lord
    and righteousness from the God of their salvation.
⁶ Such is the generation of those who seek you, O Lord,
    of those who seek your face, O God of Jacob.
⁷ Lift up your heads, O gates; and be lifted up, O everlasting doors,
    that the King of glory may come in.

⁸ Who is this King of glory?
>   The Lord, strong and mighty, the Lord, mighty in battle!

⁹ Lift up your heads, O gates;
>   lift them high, O everlasting doors, that the King of glory may come in.

¹⁰ Who is this King of glory?
>   Truly, the Lord of hosts is King of glory.

PSALM 27
NRSV

¹ The Lord is my light and my salvation; whom shall I fear?
>   The Lord is the stronghold of my life; of whom shall I be afraid?

² When evildoers assail me to devour my flesh—
>   my adversaries and foes—they shall stumble and fall.

³ Though an army encamp against me, my heart shall not fear;
>   though war rise up against me, yet I will be confident.

⁴ One thing I asked of the Lord, that will I seek after:
>   to live in the house of the Lord all the days of my life,

to behold the beauty of the Lord,
>   and to inquire in his temple.

⁵ For he will hide me in his shelter in the day of trouble;
>   he will conceal me under the cover of his tent; he will set me high on a rock.

⁶ Now my head is lifted up above my enemies all around me,
>   and I will offer in his tent sacrifices with shouts of joy;

I will sing and make melody to the Lord.
>   ⁷ Hear, O Lord, when I cry aloud, be gracious to me and answer me!

⁸ "Come," my heart says, "seek his face!"
>   Your face, Lord, do I seek.

⁹ Do not hide your face from me.
>   Do not turn your servant away in anger, you who have been my help.

Do not cast me off, do not forsake me,
>   O God of my salvation!

¹⁰ If my father and mother forsake me,
>   the Lord will take me up.

¹¹ Teach me your way, O Lord,
>   and lead me on a level path because of my enemies.

¹² Do not give me up to the will of my adversaries,
>   for false witnesses have risen against me, and they are breathing out violence.

¹³ I believe that I shall see the goodness of the Lord
>   in the land of the living.

¹⁴ Wait for the Lord; be strong,
>   and let your heart take courage; wait for the Lord!

PSALM 27
NRSV, emended

¹ God is my light and my salvation; whom shall I fear?
    God is the stronghold of my life; of whom shall I be afraid?
² When evildoers assail me to devour my flesh—
    my adversaries and foes—they shall stumble and fall.
³ Though an army encamp against me, my heart shall not fear.
    Though war rise up against me, yet I will be confident.
⁴ One thing I asked of God, that will I seek after:
    to live in the house of God all the days of my life,
to behold the beauty of God,
    and to inquire in God's temple.
⁵ For God will hide me in God's shelter in the day of trouble;
    God will conceal me under the cover of God's tent;
    God will set me high on a rock.
⁶ Now my head is lifted up above my enemies all around me,
    and I will offer in God's tent sacrifices with shouts of joy;
I will sing and make melody to God.
    ⁷ Hear, O God, when I cry aloud, be gracious to me and answer me!
⁸ "Come," my heart says, "seek God's face!"
    Your face, O God, do I seek.
⁹ Do not hide your face from me.
    Do not turn your servant away in anger, you who have been my help.
Do not cast me off, do not forsake me,
    O God of my salvation!
¹⁰ If my father and mother forsake me,
    God will take me up.
¹¹ Teach me your way, O God,
    and lead me on a level path because of my enemies.
¹² Do not give me up to the will of my adversaries,
    for false witnesses have risen against me, and they are breathing out violence.
¹³ I believe that I shall see the goodness of God
    in the land of the living.
¹⁴ Wait for God; be strong,
    let your heart take courage, wait for God!

PSALM 27
LBW, emended

¹ The LORD is my light and my salvation; whom then shall I fear?
    The LORD is the stronghold of my life; of whom shall I be afraid?
² When evildoers close in against me to devour my flesh,
    they, my foes and my enemies, will stumble and fall.
³ Though an army encamp against me, my heart will not fear.
    Though war rise up against me, in this promise I will trust.
⁴ One thing I ask of the LORD; this I seek:
    that I may dwell in the house of the LORD all the days of my life,
    to gaze upon the beauty of the LORD and to seek God in the temple.

⁵ For in the day of trouble God will give me shelter
>   and will hide me in the hidden places of the sanctuary
>   or raise me high upon a rock.

⁶ Even now my head is lifted up above my enemies who surround me.
>   Therefore I will offer sacrifice in the sanctuary, sacrifices of rejoicing;
>   I will sing and make music to the Lord.

⁷ Hear my voice, O Lord, when I call;
>   have mercy on me and answer me.

⁸ My heart speaks your message — "Seek my face."
>   Your face, O Lord, I will seek.

⁹ Hide not your face from me, turn not away from your servant in anger.
>   Cast me not away — you have been my helper; forsake me not, O God of my salvation.

¹⁰ Though my father and my mother forsake me,
>   the Lord will take me in.

¹¹ Teach me your way, O Lord;
>   lead me on a straight path, because of my oppressors.

¹² Subject me not to the will of my foes,
>   for they rise up against me, false witnesses breathing violence.

¹³ This I believe — that I will see the goodness of the Lord
>   in the land of the living!

¹⁴ Wait for the Lord and be strong.
>   Take heart and wait for the Lord!

PSALM 46
NRSV

¹ God is our refuge and strength,
>   a very present help in trouble.

² Therefore we will not fear, though the earth should change,
>   though the mountains shake in the heart of the sea;

³ though its waters roar and foam,
>   though the mountains tremble with its tumult.

⁴ There is a river whose streams make glad the city of God,
>   the holy habitation of the Most High.

⁵ God is in the midst of the city; it shall not be moved;
>   God will help it when the morning dawns.

⁶ The nations are in an uproar, the kingdoms totter;
>   he utters his voice, the earth melts.

⁷ The Lord of hosts is with us;
>   the God of Jacob is our refuge.

⁸ Come, behold the works of the Lord;
>   see what desolations he has brought on the earth.

⁹ He makes wars cease to the end of the earth;
>   he breaks the bow, and shatters the spear; he burns the shields with fire.

¹⁰ "Be still, and know that I am God!
>   I am exalted among the nations, I am exalted in the earth."

¹¹ The Lord of hosts is with us;
>   the God of Jacob is our refuge.

PSALM 46
NRSV, emended

¹ God is our refuge and strength,
    a very present help in trouble.
² Therefore we will not fear, though the earth should change,
    though the mountains shake in the heart of the sea;
³ though its waters roar and foam,
    though the mountains tremble with its tumult.
⁴ There is a river whose streams make glad the city of God,
    the holy habitation of the Most High.
⁵ God is in the midst of the city; it shall not be moved;
    God will help it when the morning dawns.
⁶ The nations are in an uproar, the empires totter;
    God's voice resounds and the earth melts.
⁷ The God of hosts is with us;
    the God of Jacob is our refuge.
⁸ Come, behold the works of God;
    see what desolations God has brought on the earth.
⁹ God makes wars cease to the end of the earth;
    God breaks the bow, and shatters the spear; God burns the shields with fire.
¹⁰ "Be still, and know that I am God!
    I am exalted among the nations, I am exalted in the earth."
¹¹ The God of hosts is with us;
    the God of Jacob is our refuge.

PSALM 46
LBW, emended

¹ God is our refuge and strength,
    a very present help in trouble.
² Therefore we will not fear, though the earth be moved,
    and though the mountains shake in the depths of the sea;
³ though its waters rage and foam,
    and though the mountains tremble with its tumult.
⁴ There is a river whose streams make glad the city of God,
    the holy habitation of the Most High.
⁵ God is in the midst of her; she shall not be shaken;
    God shall help her at the break of day.
⁶ The nations rage, and the kingdoms shake;
    God gives voice, and the earth melts away.
⁷ The Lord of hosts is with us;
    the God of Jacob is our stronghold.
⁸ Come now, regard the works of the Lord,
    what desolations God has brought upon the earth —
⁹ behold the one who makes war to cease in all the world;
    who breaks the bow, and shatters the spear, and burns the shields with fire.

10 "Be still, then, and know that I am God;
> I will be exalted among the nations; I will be exalted in the earth."

11 The Lord of hosts is with us;
> the God of Jacob is our stronghold.

PSALM 51
NRSV

1 Have mercy on me, O God, according to your steadfast love;
> according to your abundant mercy blot out my transgressions.

2 Wash me thoroughly from my iniquity, and cleanse me from my sin.
> 3 For I know my transgressions, and my sin is ever before me.

4 Against you, you alone, have I sinned, and done what is evil in your sight,
> so that you are justified in your sentence and blameless when you pass judgment.

5 Indeed, I was born guilty,
> a sinner when my mother conceived me.

6 You desire truth in the inward being;
> therefore teach me wisdom in my secret heart.

7 Purge me with hyssop, and I shall be clean;
> wash me, and I shall be whiter than snow.

8 Let me hear joy and gladness;
> let the bones that you have crushed rejoice.

9 Hide your face from my sins,
> and blot out all my iniquities.

10 Create in me a clean heart, O God,
> and put a new and right spirit within me.

11 Do not cast me away from your presence,
> and do not take your holy spirit from me.

12 Restore to me the joy of your salvation,
> and sustain in me a willing spirit.

13 Then I will teach transgressors your ways,
> and sinners will return to you.

14 Deliver me from bloodshed, O God, O God of my salvation,
> and my tongue will sing aloud of your deliverance.

15 O Lord, open my lips,
> and my mouth will declare your praise.

16 For you have no delight in sacrifice;
> if I were to give a burnt offering, you would not be pleased.

17 The sacrifice acceptable to God is a broken spirit;
> a broken and contrite heart, O God, you will not despise.

18 Do good to Zion in your good pleasure;
> rebuild the walls of Jerusalem,

19 then you will delight in right sacrifices,
> in burnt offerings and whole burnt offerings;
> then bulls will be offered on your altar.

PSALM 51
NRSV, emended

¹ Have mercy on me, O God, according to your steadfast love;
    according to your abundant mercy blot out my transgressions.
² Wash me thoroughly from my iniquity, and cleanse me from my sin.
    ³ For I know my transgressions, and my sin is ever before me.
⁴ Against you, you alone, have I sinned, and done what is evil in your sight,
    so that you are justified in your sentence and blameless when you pass judgment.
⁵ Indeed, I was born guilty,
    a sinner when my mother conceived me.
⁶ You desire truth in the inward being;
    therefore teach me wisdom in my secret heart.
⁷ Purge me with hyssop, and I shall be clean;
    wash me, and I shall be purer than snow.
⁸ Let me hear joy and gladness;
    let the bones that you have crushed rejoice.
⁹ Hide your face from my sins,
    and blot out all my iniquities.
¹⁰ Create in me a clean heart, O God,
    and put a new and right spirit within me.
¹¹ Do not cast me away from your presence,
    and do not take your holy spirit from me.
¹² Restore to me the joy of your salvation,
    and sustain in me a willing spirit.
¹³ Then I will teach transgressors your ways,
    and sinners will return to you.
¹⁴ Deliver me from bloodshed, O God, O God of my salvation,
    and my tongue will sing aloud of your deliverance.
¹⁵ O God, open my lips,
    and my mouth will declare your praise.
¹⁶ For you have no delight in sacrifice;
    if I were to give a burnt offering, you would not be pleased.
¹⁷ The sacrifice acceptable to God is a troubled spirit;
    a broken and contrite heart, O God, you will not despise.
¹⁸ Do good to Zion in your good pleasure;
    rebuild the walls of Jerusalem,
¹⁹ then you will delight in right sacrifices,
    in burnt offerings and whole burnt offerings;
    then bulls will be offered on your altar.

PSALM 51
LBW, emended

¹ Have mercy on me, O God, according to your steadfast love;
    in accord with your abundant mercy, blot out my offenses.
² Wash away all my wickedness,
    and cleanse me from my sin.

³ For I myself know my offenses,
>   and my sin is ever before me.
⁴ Against you, only you, have I sinned and done what is evil in your sight;
>   so you are justified when you speak and right in your judgment.
⁵ Indeed, I was born steeped in wickedness,
>   a sinner from my mother's womb.
⁶ Indeed, you delight in truth deep within me,
>   and would have me know wisdom deep within.
⁷ Remove my sins with hyssop, and I shall be clean;
>   wash me, and I shall be purer than snow.
⁸ Let me hear joy and gladness;
>   let the bones you have broken rejoice.
⁹ Hide your face from my sins,
>   and blot out all my wickedness.
¹⁰ Create in me a clean heart, O God,
>   and renew a right spirit within me.
¹¹ Cast me not away from your presence,
>   and take not your Holy Spirit from me.
¹² Restore to me the joy of your salvation
>   and sustain me with your bountiful Spirit.
¹³ Let me teach your ways to offenders,
>   and sinners shall be restored to you.
¹⁴ Rescue me from bloodshed, O God, O God of my salvation,
>   and my tongue shall sing of your righteousness.
¹⁵ O Lord, open my lips,
>   and my mouth shall proclaim your praise.
¹⁶ For you take no delight in sacrifice, or I would give it.
>   You are not pleased with burnt offering.
¹⁷ The sacrifice of God is a troubled spirit;
>   a troubled and broken heart, O God, you will not despise.
¹⁸ Favor Zion with your good pleasure;
>   build up the walls of Jerusalem.
¹⁹ Then you will delight in sacrifices offered in righteousness,
in burnt and whole offerings;
>   then they shall offer young bulls upon your altar.

PSALM 91
NRSV

¹ You who live in the shelter of the Most High,
>   who abide in the shadow of the Almighty, ² will say to the LORD,
"My refuge and my fortress;
>   my God, in whom I trust."
³ For he will deliver you from the snare of the fowler
>   and from the deadly pestilence;
⁴ he will cover you with his pinions, and under his wings you will find refuge;
>   his faithfulness is a shield and buckler.

⁵ You will not fear the terror of the night,
    or the arrow that flies by day,
⁶ or the pestilence that stalks in darkness,
    or the destruction that wastes at noonday.
⁷ A thousand may fall at your side,
    ten thousand at your right hand,
    but it will not come near you.
⁸ You will only look with your eyes
    and see the punishment of the wicked.
⁹ Because you have made the LORD your refuge,
    the Most High your dwelling place,
¹⁰ no evil shall befall you,
    no scourge come near your tent.
¹¹ For he will command his angels concerning you
    to guard you in all your ways.
¹² On their hands they will bear you up,
    so that you will not dash your foot against a stone.
¹³ You will tread on the lion and the adder,
    the young lion and the serpent you will trample under foot.
¹⁴ Those who love me, I will deliver;
    I will protect those who know my name.
¹⁵ When they call to me, I will answer them;
    I will be with them in trouble, I will rescue them and honor them.
¹⁶ With long life I will satisfy them,
    and show them my salvation.

PSALM 91
NRSV, emended

¹ You who live in the shelter of the Most High,
    who abide in the shadow of the Almighty, ² will say to God,
"My refuge and my fortress;
    my God, in whom I trust."
³ For God will deliver you from the snare of the fowler
    and from the deadly pestilence;
⁴ God will cover you with God's pinions, and under God's wings you will find refuge;
    God's faithfulness is a shield and buckler.
⁵ You will not fear the terror of the night,
    or the arrow that flies by day,
⁶ or the pestilence that stalks in the nighttime,
    or the destruction that wastes at noonday.
⁷ A thousand may fall at your side,
    ten thousand at your right hand,
    but it will not come near you.
⁸ You will only look with your eyes
    and see the punishment of the wicked.
⁹ Because you have made God your refuge,
    the Most High your dwelling place,

¹⁰ no evil shall befall you,
   no scourge come near your tent.
¹¹ For God will command God's angels concerning you
   to guard you in all your ways.
¹² On their hands they will bear you up,
   so that you will not dash your foot against a stone.
¹³ You will tread on the lion and the adder,
   the young lion and the serpent you will trample under foot.
¹⁴ Those who love me, I will deliver;
   I will protect those who know my name.
¹⁵ When they call to me, I will answer them;
   I will be with them in trouble, I will rescue them and honor them.
¹⁶ With long life I will satisfy them,
   and show them my salvation.

PSALM 91
LBW, emended

¹ You who dwell in the shelter of the Most High,
   who abide in the shadow of the Almighty —
² you will say to the LORD,
   "My refuge and my stronghold, my God in whom I put my trust."
³ For God will rescue you from the snare of the hunter
   and from the deadly plague.
⁴ God's wings will cover you, and you will find refuge beneath them;
   God's faithfulness will be your shield and defense.
⁵ You shall not fear any terror in the night,
   nor the arrow that flies by day;
⁶ nor the plague that stalks in the darkness,
   nor the sickness that lays waste at noon.
⁷ A thousand may fall at your side and ten thousand at your right hand,
   but it will not come near you.
⁸ You will only have to look with your eyes,
   and you will see the reward of the wicked.
⁹ Because you have made the LORD your refuge,
   and the Most High your habitation,
¹⁰ no evil will befall you,
   nor shall affliction come near your dwelling.
¹¹ For God will give the angels charge over you,
   to guard you in all of your ways.
¹² Upon their hands they will bear you up,
   lest you strike your foot against a stone.
¹³ You will tread upon the lion cub and viper;
   you will trample down the lion and the serpent.
¹⁴ Those who love me, I will deliver;
   I will uphold them, because they know my name.
¹⁵ They will call me, and I will answer them;
   I will be with them in trouble; I will rescue and honor them.

[16] With long life will I satisfy them,
    and show them my salvation.

PSALM 95
NRSV

[1] Oh, come, let us sing to the Lord;
    let us make a joyful noise to the rock of our salvation!
[2] Let us come into his presence with thanksgiving;
    let us make a joyful noise to him with songs of praise!
[3] For the Lord is a great God,
    and a great King above all gods.
[4] In his hand are the depths of the earth;
    the heights of the mountains are his also.
[5] The sea is his, for he made it,
    and the dry land, which his hands have formed.
[6] Oh, come, let us worship and bow down,
    let us kneel before the Lord, our Maker!
[7] For he is our God,
    and we are the people of his pasture, and the sheep of his hand.
Oh, that today you would listen to his voice!
    [8] Do not harden your hearts, as at Meribah, as on the day at Massah in the wilderness,
[9] when your ancestors tested me,
    and put me to the proof, though they had seen my work.
[10] For forty years I loathed that generation and said,
    "They are a people whose hearts go astray, and they do not regard my ways."
[11] Therefore in my anger I swore,
    "They shall not enter my rest."

PSALM 95
NRSV, emended

[1] Oh, come, let us sing to God;
    let us make a joyful noise to the rock of our salvation!
[2] Let us come into God's presence with thanksgiving;
    let us make a joyful noise to God with songs of praise!
[3] For God is a great God,
    and a great Ruler above all gods.
[4] In God's hand are the depths of the earth;
    the heights of the mountains are God's also.
[5] The sea is God's, for God made it,
    and the dry land, which God's hands have formed.
[6] Oh, come, let us worship and bow down,
    let us kneel before God, our Maker!
[7] For God is our God,
    and we are the people of God's pasture, and the sheep of his hand.
Oh, that today you would listen to God's voice!

⁸ Do not harden your hearts, as at Meribah, as on the day at Massah in the wilderness,
⁹ when your ancestors tested me,
    and put me to the proof, though they had seen my work.
¹⁰ For forty years I loathed that generation and said,
    "They are a people whose hearts go astray, and they do not regard my ways."
¹¹ Therefore in my anger I swore,
    "They shall not enter my rest."

PSALM 95
LBW, emended

¹ Come, let us sing to the Lord;
    let us shout for joy to the rock of our salvation.
² Let us come before God's presence with thanksgiving
    and raise a loud shout to the Lord with psalms.
³ For you, Lord, are a great God,
    and a great ruler above all gods.
⁴ In your hand are the caverns of the earth;
    the heights of the hills are also yours.
⁵ The sea is yours, for you made it;
    and your hands have molded the dry land.
⁶ Come, let us worship and bow down;
    let us kneel before the Lord our maker.
⁷ For the Lord is our God,
    and we are the people of God's pasture and the sheep of God's hand.
Oh, that today we would hear God's voice!
    ⁸ "Harden not your hearts, as at Meribah, as on that day at Massah in the desert.
⁹ There they tested me, your ancestors;
    they put me to the test, though they had seen my works.
¹⁰ Forty years I loathed that generation, saying,
    'The heart of this people goes astray; they do not know my ways.'
¹¹ Indeed I swore in my anger,
    'They shall never come into my rest.'"

PSALM 100
NRSV

¹ Make a joyful noise to the Lord, all the earth.
    ² Worship the Lord with gladness; come into his presence with singing.
³ Know that the Lord is God. It is he that made us,
    and we are his; we are his people, and the sheep of his pasture.
⁴ Enter his gates with thanksgiving, and his courts with praise.
    Give thanks to him, bless his name.
⁵ For the Lord is good; his steadfast love endures forever,
    and his faithfulness to all generations.

PSALM 100
NRSV, emended

¹ Make a joyful noise to God, all the earth.
    ² Worship God with gladness; come into God's presence with singing.
³ Know that the Sovereign is God. It is God that made us,
    and we are God's; we are God's people, and the sheep of God's pasture.
⁴ Enter God's gates with thanksgiving, and enter God's courts with praise.
    Give thanks to God, and bless God's name.
⁵ For God is good; God's steadfast love endures forever,
    and God's faithfulness to all generations.

PSALM 100
LBW, emended

¹Make a joyful noise to the Lord, all you lands!
    ²Serve the Lord with gladness; come into God's presence with a song.
³Know that the Lord alone is God, our maker to whom we belong;
    we are God's people, and the sheep of God's pasture.
⁴ Enter the temple gates with thanksgiving and its courts with praise;
    give thanks and bless God's holy name.
⁵ Good indeed is the Lord, whose mercy is everlasting,
    whose faithfulness endures from age to age.

PSALM 121
NRSV

¹ I lift up my eyes to the hills—
    from where will my help come?
² My help comes from the Lord,
    who made heaven and earth.
³ He will not let your foot be moved;
    he who keeps you will not slumber.
⁴ He who keeps Israel
    will neither slumber nor sleep.
⁵ The Lord is your keeper;
    the Lord is your shade at your right hand.
⁶ The sun shall not strike you by day,
    nor the moon by night.
⁷ The Lord will keep you from all evil;
    he will keep your life.
⁸ The Lord will keep your going out and your coming in
    from this time on and forevermore.

PSALM 121
NRSV, emended

¹ I lift up my eyes to the hills—
    from where will my help come?
² My help comes from God,
    who made heaven and earth.
³ God will not let your foot be moved;
    God who keeps you will not slumber.
⁴ God who keeps Israel
    will neither slumber nor sleep.
⁵ God is your keeper;
    God is your shade at your side.
⁶ The sun shall not strike you by day,
    nor the moon by night.
⁷ God will keep you from all evil;
    God will keep your life.
⁸ God will keep your going out and your coming in
    from this time on and forevermore.

PSALM 121
LBW, emended

¹ I lift up my eyes to the hills;
    from where will my help come?
² My help comes from the Lord,
    maker of heaven and earth.
³ The Lord will not let your foot be moved
    nor will the one who keeps you slumber.
⁴ Behold, the keeper of Israel
    will neither slumber nor sleep;
⁵ the Lord is your keeper;
    the Lord is your shade at your right hand;
⁶ the sun will not strike you by day,
    nor the moon by night.
⁷ The Lord will keep you from all evil
    and will keep your life.
⁸ The Lord will keep your going out and your coming in
    from this time forth forevermore.

PSALM 130
NRSV

¹ Out of the depths I cry to you, O Lord.
    ² Lord, hear my voice!
Let your ears be attentive to the voice of my supplications!
        ³ If you, O Lord, should mark iniquities, Lord, who could stand?

⁴ But there is forgiveness with you, so that you may be revered.
    ⁵ I wait for the LORD, my soul waits, and in his word I hope;
⁶ my soul waits for the Lord more than those who watch for the morning,
    more than those who watch for the morning.
⁷ O Israel, hope in the LORD!
    For with the LORD there is steadfast love,
and with him is great power to redeem.
    ⁸ It is he who will redeem Israel from all its iniquities.

PSALM 130
NRSV, emended

¹ Out of the depths I cry to you, O God.
    ² O God, hear my voice!
Let your ears be attentive to the voice of my supplications!
    ³ If you, O God, should mark iniquities, who could stand?
⁴ But there is forgiveness with you, so that you may be revered.
    ⁵ I wait for God, my soul waits, and in God's word I hope;
⁶ my soul waits for God more than those who watch for the morning,
    more than those who watch for the morning.
⁷ O Israel, hope in God!
    For with God there is steadfast love.
With God is great power to redeem;
    ⁸ It is God who will redeem Israel from all its iniquities.

PSALM 130
LBW, emended

¹ Out of the depths I cry to you, O LORD;
    ² O Lord, hear my voice!
Let your ears be attentive to the voice of my supplication.
    ³ If you were to keep watch over sins, O LORD, who could stand?
⁴ Yet with you is forgiveness,
    in order that you may be feared.
⁵ I wait for the LORD; my soul waits;
    in God's word is my hope.
⁶ My soul waits for the Lord more than those who keep watch for the morning,
    more than those who keep watch for the morning.
⁷ O Israel, wait for the LORD,
    for with the LORD there is steadfast love;
with the LORD there is plenteous redemption.
    ⁸ For the LORD will redeem Israel from all their sins.

PSALM 133
NRSV

¹ How very good and pleasant it is
    when kindred live together in unity!
² It is like the precious oil on the head,
    running down upon the beard,
on the beard of Aaron,
    running down over the collar of his robes.
³ It is like the dew of Hermon,
    which falls on the mountains of Zion.
For there the LORD ordained his blessing,
    life forevermore.

PSALM 133
NRSV, emended

¹ How very good and pleasant it is
    when kindred live together in unity!
² It is like the precious oil on the head,
    running down upon the beard,
upon the beard of Aaron,
    running down over the collar of his robes.
³ It is like the dew of Hermon,
    which falls on the mountains of Zion.
For there God ordained the blessing,
    the blessing of life forevermore.

PSALM 133
LBW, emended

¹ How good and how pleasant indeed,
    when kindred live together in unity!
² It is like fine oil upon the head,
    flowing down upon the beard,
upon the beard of Aaron,
    flowing down upon the collar of his robe.
³ It is like the dew of Hermon
    flowing down upon the hills of Zion.
For there the Lord has commanded the blessing:
    life into eternity.

PSALM 141
NRSV

¹ I call upon you, O LORD; come quickly to me;
    give ear to my voice when I call to you.
² Let my prayer be counted as incense before you,
    and the lifting up of my hands as an evening sacrifice.

³ Set a guard over my mouth, O Lord;
   keep watch over the door of my lips.
⁴ Do not turn my heart to any evil, to busy myself with wicked deeds
in company with those who work iniquity;
   do not let me eat of their delicacies.
⁵ Let the righteous strike me;
   let the faithful correct me.
Never let the oil of the wicked anoint my head,
   for my prayer is continually against their wicked deeds.
⁶ When they are given over to those who shall condemn them,
   then they shall learn that my words were pleasant.
⁷ Like a rock that one breaks apart and shatters on the land,
   so shall their bones be strewn at the mouth of Sheol.
⁸ But my eyes are turned toward you, O God, my Lord;
   in you I seek refuge; do not leave me defenseless.
⁹ Keep me from the trap that they have laid for me,
   and from the snares of evildoers.
¹⁰ Let the wicked fall into their own nets,
   while I alone escape.

PSALM 141
NRSV, emended

¹ I call upon you, O God; come quickly to me;
   give ear to my voice when I call to you.
² Let my prayer be counted as incense before you,
   and the lifting up of my hands as an evening sacrifice.
³ Set a guard over my mouth, O God;
   keep watch over the door of my lips.
⁴ Do not turn my heart to any evil, to busy myself with wicked deeds
with those who work iniquity;
   do not let me eat of their delicacies.
⁵ Let the righteous strike me;
   let the faithful correct me.
Never let the oil of the wicked anoint my head,
   for my prayer is continually against their wicked deeds.
⁶ When they are given over to those who shall condemn them,
   then they shall learn that my words were pleasant.
⁷ Like a rock that one breaks apart and shatters on the land,
   so shall their bones be strewn at the mouth of Sheol.
⁸ But my eyes are turned toward you, O God, my God;
   in you I seek refuge; do not leave me defenseless.
⁹ Keep me from the trap that they have laid for me,
   and from the snares of evildoers.
¹⁰ Let the wicked fall into their own nets,
   while I alone escape.

PSALM 141
LBW, emended

¹ O LORD, I call to you; come to me quickly;
    hear my voice when I cry to you.
² Let my prayer rise before you as incense,
    the lifting up of my hands as the evening sacrifice.
³ Set a watch before my mouth, O LORD,
    and guard the door of my lips;
⁴ let not my heart incline to any evil thing.
    Let me not take part in evil deeds with evildoers, nor eat of their sweet foods.
⁵ Let the righteous strike me down with steadfast love;
their rebukes, as oil upon the head, are not to be refused.
    Yet my prayers are still against the deeds of the wicked.
⁶ Let their rulers be thrown down upon the stones,
    that they may hear my words, for they are sweet.
⁷ Just as one who plows breaks through the earth,
    so let their bones be scattered at the mouth of the grave.
⁸ But my eyes are turned to you, Lord GOD;
    in you I take refuge; strip me not of my life.
⁹ Guard me from the grasp of the trap they have laid for me
    and from the snares of evildoers.
¹⁰ Let the wicked fall into their own nets,
    while I alone pass through.

RENEWING ✠ WORSHIP

Daily Lectionary

DAILY LECTIONARY
related to the Revised Common Lectionary

The following table of readings is an excerpt from a draft of a project currently underway by the Consultation on Common Texts, the ecumenical group that prepared the Revised Common Lectionary for release in 1992. The draft is currently under review by denominational members of the group, and is subject to further revision before its projected release in 2005. Responses to this proposal in these provisional resources will help determine its potential for use in longer-term Lutheran resources.

The foundational premise of this set of daily readings is their relationship to the Sunday lectionary. The readings are chosen so that the days leading up to Sunday (Thursday through Saturday) prepare for the Sunday readings. The days flowing out from Sunday (Monday through Wednesday) reflect upon the Sunday readings. From the whole body of readings for a week, selections may be made for the local context, especially when this lectionary is used more occasionally.

The excerpt presented here includes the readings from Advent through Pentecost of year A, the optimal time for provisional use and testing of the materials in this volume. Longer-term resources, if this approach is affirmed, would include the full three-year cycle of readings.

ADVENT

FIRST SUNDAY OF ADVENT

Preparation for Sunday

Thursday
Daniel 9:15-19
A plea for forgiveness
James 4:1-10
A plea for God's grace and human humility

Friday
Genesis 6:1-10
The righteousness of Noah
Hebrews 11:1-7
Noah acts in faith

Saturday
Genesis 6:11-22
The flood is coming
Matthew 24:1-22
The day of the Lord is coming

Daily
Psalm 122
Gladness in the LORD's house

First Sunday of Advent

Isaiah 2:1-5
War transformed into peace
Psalm 122
Gladness in the LORD's house
Romans 13:11-14
Salvation is near; wake from sleep
Matthew 24:36-44
The sudden coming of salvation

Reflection on Sunday

Monday
Genesis 8:1-19
The obedience of Noah
Romans 6:1-11
Dying and rising with Christ through baptism

Tuesday
Genesis 9:1-17
The sign of the rainbow
Hebrews 11:32-40
By faith, Gideon, Barak, and many women . . .

Wednesday
Isaiah 54:1-10
God will save the people
Matthew 24:23-35
The end is coming

Daily
Psalm 124
We have escaped like a bird

SECOND SUNDAY OF ADVENT

Preparation for Sunday

Thursday
Isaiah 4:2-6
God's promised glory for the survivors in Zion
Acts 1:12-26
Beginnings of the apostolic ministry

Friday
Isaiah 30:19-26
God's promise to be gracious to Zion
Acts 13:16-25
Paul's testimony concerning John the Baptist

Saturday
Isaiah 40:1-11
A voice crying in the wilderness
John 1:19-28
John the Baptist concerning his own ministry

Daily
Psalm 72:1-7, 18-19
The righteous shall flourish

Second Sunday of Advent

Isaiah 11:1-10
A ruler brings justice and peace
Psalm 72:1-7, 18-19
The righteous shall flourish
Romans 15:4-13
Living in harmony
Matthew 3:1-12
Prepare the way of the Lord

Reflection on Sunday

Monday
Isaiah 24:1-16a
Judgment is coming, but glorify God
1 Thessalonians 4:1-12
A solemn warning by the apostle Paul

Tuesday
Isaiah 41:14-20
God will not forget the poor of Israel
Romans 15:14-21
Gentiles are also called to the obedience of faith

Wednesday
Genesis 15:1-18
God's covenant with Abram
Matthew 12:33-37
A good tree bears good fruit

Daily
Psalm 21
God comes with judgment and strength

THIRD SUNDAY OF ADVENT

Preparation for Sunday

Thursday
Ruth 1:6-18
Ruth's fidelity to the people of the covenant
2 Peter 3:1-10
The promise of the Lord's coming

Friday
Ruth 4:13-17
God's fidelity toward Ruth and her posterity
2 Peter 3:11-18
Prepare for the Lord's coming

Saturday
1 Samuel 2:1-8
Hannah's canticle in praise of God's fidelity
Luke 3:1-19
The proclamation of John the Baptist

Daily
Psalm 146:5-10
God lifts up those bowed down

Third Sunday of Advent

Isaiah 35:1-10
The desert blooms
Psalm 146:5-10   or   Luke 1:47-55
God lifts up those bowed down   *My spirit rejoices in God*
James 5:7-10
Patience until the Lord's coming
Matthew 11:2-11
The forerunner of Christ

Reflection on Sunday

Monday
Isaiah 29:17-24
The infirm will be healed
Acts 5:12-16
Many people healed by the apostles

Tuesday
Ezekiel 47:1-12
The wilderness will flower
Jude 17-24
Prepare for the Lord's coming

Wednesday
Zechariah 8:1-17
God's promise to Zion
Matthew 8:14-17, 28-34
Jesus heals

Daily
Psalm 42
Hope in God

FOURTH SUNDAY OF ADVENT

Readings for Monday through Wednesday after the fourth Sunday of Advent are provided for use if necessary. Beginning with December 22, the dated readings on the following pages may be used.

Preparation for Sunday

Thursday
2 Samuel 7:1-17
God will build you a house
Galatians 3:23-29
God's Son, sent in the fullness of time

Friday
2 Samuel 7:18-29
David's prayer for God's faithfulness toward Israel
Galatians 4:8-20
The apostles' concern for the Galatian church

Saturday
Genesis 37:1-11
Joseph dreams he will rule over his brothers
John 3:31-36
The One who comes from above

Daily
Psalm 80:1-7, 17-19
Show the light of your countenance

> *Fourth Sunday of Advent*
>
> Isaiah 7:10-16
> *The sign of Immanuel*
> Psalm 80:1-7, 17-19
> *Show the light of your countenance*
> Romans 1:1-7
> *Paul's greeting to the church at Rome*
> Matthew 1:18-25
> *Our God near at hand*

Reflection on Sunday

Monday
Genesis 17:15-22
God promises Sarah a son
Galatians 4:1-7
Paul writes of Jesus' birth

Tuesday
Genesis 21:1-21
God saves Hagar and Ishmael
Galatians 4:21—5:1
Two women, two covenants, one freedom

Wednesday
Genesis 37:2-11
Joseph dreams
Matthew 1:1-17
Jesus' genealogy

Daily
1 Samuel 2:1-10
Canticle of Hannah

CHRISTMAS

DAYS AROUND CHRISTMAS DAY

December 22
Isaiah 33:17-22
The Lord will save us
Revelation 22:6-7, 18-20
See, I am coming soon

December 23
2 Samuel 7:18, 23-29
Your servant will be blessed
Galatians 3:6-14
The promise of the Spirit

December 24 (morning only)
Isaiah 60:1-6
Arise, shine!
Luke 1:67-80
The song of Zechariah

Daily
Luke 1:46-55
My soul gives glory to God

Birth of Our Lord I

Isaiah 9:2-7
A child is born for us
Psalm 96
Let the earth be glad
Titus 2:11-14
The grace of God has appeared
Luke 2:1-14 [15-20]
God with us

Birth of Our Lord II

Isaiah 62:6-12
God comes to restore the people
Psalm 97
Light springs up for the righteous
Titus 3:4-7
Saved through water and the Spirit
Luke 2:[1-7] 8-20
Birth of the messiah revealed to shepherds

Birth of Our Lord III

Isaiah 52:7-10
Heralds announce God's salvation
Psalm 98
The victory of our God
Hebrews 1:1-4 [5-12]
God has spoken by a son
John 1:1-14
The Word became flesh

December 26
Wisdom 4:7-15
The righteous are rewarded
Acts 7:59—8:8
Stephen is stoned to death

December 27
Proverbs 8:22-30
Wisdom's part in creation
1 John 5:1-12
Whoever loves God loves God's child

December 28
Isaiah 49:13-23
God comforts the suffering
Matthew 18:1-14
Become like a child

Daily
Psalm 148
God's splendor is over earth and heaven

First Sunday after Christmas Day, December 26–31

Isaiah 63:7-9
Israel saved by God's own presence
Psalm 148
God's splendor is over earth and heaven
Hebrews 2:10-18
Christ frees humankind
Matthew 2:13-23
The slaughter of innocent children

DAYS OF CHRISTMAS

Daily
Psalm 20
Answer us when we call

December 29
Jeremiah 31:15-22
Weeping in Ramah
Luke 19:41-44
Jesus weeps over Jerusalem

December 30
Isaiah 26:1-9
Trust in God forever
2 Corinthians 4:16—5:5
We are ambassadors for Christ

December 31 New Year's Eve
1 Kings 3:5-14
God grants a discerning mind
Psalm 102:24-28
God's years have no end
2 Corinthians 5:16—6:2
Everything old passes away
John 8:12-19
I am the light

January 1 New Year's Day
Ecclesiastes 3:1-13
To everything a season
Psalm 8
How exalted is your name
Revelation 21:1-6a
New heaven and new earth
Matthew 25:31-46
Judgment

January 1 Name of Jesus
Numbers 6:22-27
The Aaronic blessing
Psalm 8
How exalted is your name
Galatians 4:4-7
We are no longer slaves
or Philippians 2:5-11
God takes on human form
Luke 2:15-21
The child is named Jesus

January 2
Genesis 12:1-7
Abram and Sarai
Hebrews 11:1-12
By faith . . .

Second Sunday after Christmas Day, January 2–5

Jeremiah 31:7-14   *or*
Joy as God's scattered flock gathers
Psalm 147:12-20   *or*
Praising God in Zion
Ephesians 1:3-14
The will of God made known in Christ
John 1:[1-9] 10-18
God with us

Sirach 24:1-12
Wisdom lives among God's people
Wisdom of Solomon 10:15-21
Praising the holy name

EPIPHANY

DAYS AROUND EPIPHANY

Readings through January 9 are provided for use if necessary. When the Epiphany of Our Lord is transferred to the preceding Sunday, January 2–5, the dated readings below may be used through the week that follows. When the Baptism of Our Lord falls on January 11, 12, or 13, the corresponding preparation readings on the following page are used after January 9.

January 3
Genesis 28:10-22
Jacob's ladder
Hebrews 11:13-22
By faith . . .

January 4
Exodus 3:1-5
The burning bush
Hebrews 11:23-31
By faith. . .

January 5
Joshua 1:1-9
Be strong
Hebrews 11:32—12:2
Surrounded by a cloud of witnesses

Daily
Psalm 72
Prayers for the king

Epiphany of Our Lord, January 6

Isaiah 60:1-6
Nations come to the light
Psalm 72:1-7, 10-14
All shall bow down
Ephesians 3:1-12
The gospel's promise for all
Matthew 2:1-12
Christ revealed to the nations

January 7
1 Kings 10:1-13
Gifts to Solomon from Sheba
Ephesians 3:14-21
Knowing the love of Christ

January 8
1 Kings 10:14-25
Solomon's splendor
Ephesians 4:7, 11-16
Gifts according to Christ

January 9
Micah 5:2-9
One who is to rule Israel
Luke 13:31-35
Jerusalem that kills the prophets

Daily
Psalm 72
Prayer for the king

BAPTISM OF OUR LORD
Sunday 1, time after Epiphany

Preparation for Sunday

Thursday
1 Samuel 3:1-9
Samuel, a boy, says "Here I am"
Acts 9:1-9
Saul is given a vision of Jesus

Friday
1 Samuel 3:10—4:1a
Samuel receives the word of God at Shiloh
Acts 9:10-19a
Ananias receives Saul into the church

Saturday
1 Samuel 7:3-17
Samuel guides Israel to peace
Acts 9:19b-31
Paul introduced to the church in Jerusalem

Daily
Psalm 29
The voice of God upon the waters

Baptism of Our Lord, Sunday 1, time after Epiphany

Isaiah 42:1-9
The servant of God brings justice
Psalm 29
The voice of God upon the waters
Acts 10:34-43
Jesus' ministry after his baptism
Matthew 3:13-17
Christ revealed as God's servant

Reflection on Sunday

Monday
Genesis 35:1-15
God calls and blesses Jacob
Acts 10:44-48
God calls Gentiles to be baptized

Tuesday
Jeremiah 1:4-10
God calls Jeremiah
Acts 8:4-13
Philip preaches and baptizes

Wednesday
Isaiah 51:1-16
God saves the people through water
Matthew 12:15-21
The words of Isaiah applied to Jesus

Daily
Psalm 89:5-37
God anoints David to be a son

SUNDAY 2
Time after Epiphany

Preparation for Sunday

Thursday
Isaiah 22:15-25
God replaces disobedient leaders
Galatians 1:11-24
Paul reflects on his calling into discipleship

Friday
Genesis 27:30-38
Jacob receives Esau's blessing
Acts 1:1-5
The promise of the Holy Spirit

Saturday
1 Kings 19:19-21
Elijah calls Elisha to follow him
Luke 5:1-11
Jesus calls the first disciples

Daily
Psalm 40:1-11
Doing the will of God

Sunday 2, time after Epiphany

Isaiah 49:1-7
The servant brings light to the nations
Psalm 40:1-11
Doing the will of God
1 Corinthians 1:1-9
Paul's greeting to the church at Corinth
John 1:29-42
Christ revealed as the Lamb of God

Reflection on Sunday

Monday
Exodus 12:1-13, 21-28
The passover lamb
Acts 8:26-40
Philip teaches about the lamb

Tuesday
Isaiah 53:1-12
The one like a lamb
Hebrews 10:1-4
Animal sacrifices cannot take away sins

Wednesday
Isaiah 48:12-21
God saves the people through water
Matthew 9:14-17
Christ, the bridegroom, the new wine

Daily
Psalm 40:6-17
Not sacrifice, but divine mercy

SUNDAY 3
Time after Epiphany

Preparation for Sunday

Thursday
1 Samuel 1:1-20
The call of the prophet Samuel
Galatians 2:1-10
Paul proclaims his authority

Friday
1 Samuel 9:27—10:8
Saul anointed by Samuel as king
Galatians 1:11-24
The divine origin of Paul's gospel

Saturday
1 Samuel 15:34—16:13
David anointed as king to replace King Saul
Luke 5:27-32
The call of Levi

Daily
Psalm 27:1, 4-9
The LORD is light

Sunday 3, time after Epiphany

Isaiah 9:1-4
Light shines for those in darkness
Psalm 27:1, 4-9
The LORD is light
1 Corinthians 1:10-18
An appeal for unity in the gospel
Matthew 4:12-23
Christ revealed as a prophet

Reflection on Sunday

Monday
Judges 6:11-24
God calls Gideon to lead the people
Ephesians 5:6-14
Live as children of the light

Tuesday
Judges 7:12-22
God leads Gideon to victory
Philippians 2:12-18
Call to shine like stars

Wednesday
Genesis 49:1-2, 8-13, 21-26
Judah, Zebulun, Naphtali blessed
Luke 1:67-79
Christ, the light dawning

Daily
Psalm 27:7-14
God our light, our victory

SUNDAY 4
Time after Epiphany

Preparation for Sunday

Thursday
Deuteronomy 16:18—17:1
Pursue only justice
1 Peter 3:8-12
Repay evil with a blessing

Friday
Deuteronomy 24:17—25:4
Do not deprive others of justice
1 Timothy 5:17-24
Good works are conspicuous

Saturday
Micah 3:1-4
Should you not know justice?
John 13:31-35
The new commandment

Daily
Psalm 15
Abiding on God's holy hill

Sunday 4, time after Epiphany

Micah 6:1-8
The offering of justice, kindness, humility
Psalm 15
Abiding on God's holy hill
1 Corinthians 1:18-31
Christ crucified, the wisdom and power of God
Matthew 5:1-12
The teaching of Christ: Beatitudes

Reflection on Sunday

Monday
Ruth 1:1-18
Ruth, one of the poor
Philemon 1-25
Concerning the slave Onesimus

Tuesday
Ruth 2:1-16
Ruth, one of the hungry
James 5:1-6
A warning to the ungenerous

Wednesday
Ruth 3:1-13; 4:13-22
Ruth, one of the blessed
Luke 6:17-26
The Beatitudes in Luke

Daily
Psalm 37:1-17
God will bless the righteous

SUNDAY 5
Time after Epiphany

Preparation for Sunday

Thursday
Deuteronomy 4:1-14
The discipline of faith
1 John 5:1-5
God's children obey God's commandments

Friday
Isaiah 29:1-12
Hunger that goes unsatisfied
James 3:13-18
A gentle life born of wisdom

Saturday
Isaiah 29:13-16
Hearts far from God
Mark 7:1-8
The inadequacy of "lip" religion

Daily
Psalm 112:1-9 [10]
Light shines in the darkness

Sunday 5, time after Epiphany

Isaiah 58:1-9a [9b-12]
The fast God chooses
Psalm 112:1-9 [10]
Light shines in the darkness
1 Corinthians 2:1-12 [13-16]
God's wisdom revealed through the Spirit
Matthew 5:13-20
The teaching of Christ: salt and light

Reflection on Sunday

Monday
2 Kings 22:3-20
Huldah urges Josiah to keep the law
Romans 11:2-10
A remnant remains faithful

Tuesday
2 Kings 23:1-8; 21-25
King Josiah keeps the law
2 Corinthians 4:1-12
Christ, the light

Wednesday
Proverbs 6:6-23
The law is a lamp
John 8:12-30
You are the light of the world

Daily
Psalm 119:105-112
The law is light

SUNDAY 6
Time after Epiphany

Preparation for Sunday

Thursday
Genesis 26:1-5
Abraham obeys God's commandments
James 1:12-16
God tempts no one

Friday
Leviticus 26:34-46
God's covenant remembered
1 John 2:7-17
Old and new commandments

Saturday
Deuteronomy 30:1-9a
God's fidelity assured
Matthew 15:1-9
God's commandments and religious tradition

Daily
Psalm 119:1-8
Happy are those who walk in the law

Sunday 6, time after Epiphany

Deuteronomy 30:15-2
Choose life
Psalm 119:1-8
Happy are those who walk in the law
1 Corinthians 3:1-9
God gives the growth
Matthew 5:21-37
The teaching of Christ: forgiveness

or

Sirach 15:15-20
Choose between life and death

Reflection on Sunday

Monday
Exodus 20:1-21
The ten commandments
James 1:2-8
Facing trials

Tuesday
Deuteronomy 23:21—24:4, 10-15
Israel's communal laws
James 2:1-13
The law, judgment and mercy

Wednesday
Proverbs 2:1-15
The way of wisdom
Matthew 19:1-12
Jesus teaches about divorce

Daily
Psalm 119:9-16
I delight in the law

SUNDAY 7
Time after Epiphany

Preparation for Sunday

Thursday
Exodus 22:21-27
Compassion for neighbors
1 Corinthians 10:23—11:1
Do not seek your own advantage

Friday
Leviticus 6:1-7
Sin against a neighbor
Galatians 5:2-6
Faith working through love

Saturday
Leviticus 24:10-23
An eye for an eye
Matthew 7:1-12
The golden rule

Daily
Psalm 119:33-40
Walking in the path of the law

Sunday 7, time after Epiphany

Leviticus 19:1-2, 9-18
Acts of mercy and justice
Psalm 119:33-40
Walking in the path of the law
1 Corinthians 3:10-11, 16-23
Allegiance to Christ, not human leaders
Matthew 5:38-48
The teaching of Christ: love

Reflection on Sunday

Monday
Proverbs 25:11-22
Caring for the enemy
Romans 12:9-21
Caring for the enemy

Tuesday
Genesis 31:1-7, 17-26, 44-50
Laban and Jacob reconcile
Hebrews 12:14-16
Pursue peace with everyone

Wednesday
Proverbs 3:27-35
Regard for neighbors
Luke 18:18-30
Give to the poor (the rich young ruler)

Daily
Psalm 119:57-64
Keeping the law in spite of the wicked

SUNDAY 8
Time after Epiphany

Preparation for Sunday

Thursday
Proverbs 12:22-28
Anxiety burdens the heart
Philippians 2:19-24
Concern for our own interests

Friday
Isaiah 26:1-6
Trust in God
Philippians 2:25-30
Paul overcomes anxiety

Saturday
Isaiah 31:1-9
Misplaced trust
Luke 11:14-23
Trust that disappoints

Daily
Psalm 131
A child upon its mother's breast

Sunday 8, time after Epiphany

Isaiah 49:8-16a
God's motherly compassion
Psalm 131
A child upon its mother's breast
1 Corinthians 4:1-5
Servants accountable to God
Matthew 6:24-34
The teaching of Christ: trust in God

Reflection on Sunday

Monday
Deuteronomy 32:1-14
God's care for the chosen people
Hebrews 10:32-39
Confidence that rewards

Tuesday
1 Kings 17:1-16
God feeds the widow
1 Corinthians 4:6-21
The life of an apostle

Wednesday
Isaiah 66:7-13
God as a nursing mother
Luke 12:22-31
Do not worry

Daily
Psalm 104
God cares for all the earth

TRANSFIGURATION OF OUR LORD
Sunday before Lent

Preparation for Sunday

Thursday
Exodus 6:2-9
God promises deliverance through Moses
Hebrews 8:1-7
Moses remembers God's instruction

Friday
Exodus 19:9b-25
Israel consecrated at Sinai
Hebrews 11:23-28
Moses anticipates Christ

Saturday
1 Kings 21:20-29
Elijah pronounces God's sentence
Mark 9:9-13
The coming of Elijah

Daily
Psalm 2
The one begotten of God

Transfiguration of Our Lord

Exodus 24:12-18
Moses enters the cloud of God's glory
Psalm 2
The one begotten of God
2 Peter 1:16-21
Shining with the glory of God
Matthew 17:1-9
Christ revealed as God's beloved Son

Reflection on Sunday

Monday
Exodus 33:7-23
Moses sees God's glory
Acts 7:30-34
Moses on holy ground

Tuesday
1 Kings 19:1-3, 9-18
Elijah hears God
Romans 11:1-6
Elijah pleads with God

Daily
Psalm 78:17-20, 52-55
Israel led to God's holy mountain

DAILY LECTIONARY 81

LENT

FIRST SUNDAY IN LENT

Ash Wednesday

Joel 2:1-2, 12-17   or   Isaiah 58:1-12
Return to God   *The fast that God chooses*
Psalm 51:1-17
Plea for mercy
2 Corinthians 5:20b—6:10
Now is the day of salvation
Matthew 6:1-6, 16-21
The practice of faith

Preparation for Sunday

Thursday
Jonah 3:1-10
Nineveh repents
Romans 1:1-7
Appointed to preach the good news of Christ

Friday
Jonah 4:1-11
God mercifully reproves Jonah
Romans 1:8-17
Live by faith

Saturday
Isaiah 58:1-12
The fast that God chooses
Matthew 18:6-14
Temptation and forgiveness

Daily
Psalm 51
Create in me a clean heart

First Sunday in Lent

Genesis 2:15-17; 3:1-7
Eating of the tree of knowledge
Psalm 32
Mercy embraces us
Romans 5:12-19
Death came, life comes
Matthew 4:1-11
The temptation of Jesus

Reflection on Sunday

Monday
1 Kings 19:1-18
An angel feeds Elijah in the wilderness
Hebrews 2:10-18
Christ goes before us in suffering

Tuesday
Genesis 4:1-16
God protects Cain
Hebrews 4:14—5:10
Christ was tempted as we are

Wednesday
Exodus 34:1-9, 27-28
God's revelation of mercy
Matthew 18:6-14
Temptation and forgiveness

Daily
Psalm 32
Mercy embraces us

SECOND SUNDAY IN LENT

Preparation for Sunday

Thursday
Isaiah 51:1-3
Eden's fulfillment for the children of the promise
2 Timothy 1:3-7
Faith handed down from faithful mothers

Friday
Micah 7:18-20
Praise for the faithfulness of Abraham
Romans 3:21-31
Paul relates law and faith

Saturday
Isaiah 51:4-8
God's word means justice for all
John 8:48-59
Even before Abraham, Jesus the Christ

Daily
Psalm 121
The LORD watches over you

Second Sunday in Lent

Genesis 12:1-4a
The blessing of God upon Abram
Psalm 121
The LORD watches over you
Romans 4:1-5, 13-17
The promise to those of Abraham's faith
John 3:1-17
The mission of Christ: saving the world

Reflection on Sunday

Monday
Numbers 21:4-9
Moses lifts up the serpent
Hebrews 3:1-6
Moses the servant, Christ the son

Tuesday
Isaiah 65:17-25
God promises a new creation
Romans 4:6-13
Abraham's descendants inherit a new world

Wednesday
Ezekiel 36:22-32
God will renew the people
John 8:1-11
Jesus does not condemn the sinner

Daily
Psalm 128
God promises life

THIRD SUNDAY IN LENT

Preparation for Sunday

Thursday
Exodus 16:1-8
Israel complains of hunger in the wilderness
Colossians 1:15-23
Christ the incarnate reconciliation of all things

Friday
Exodus 16:9-21
God gives manna and quail
Ephesians 2:11-21
In Christ God reconciles Jew and Gentile

Saturday
Exodus 16:27-35
Celebrating God's gifts of food and drink
John 4:1-6
Jesus travels to Jacob's well in Samaria

Daily
Psalm 95
The rock of our salvation

Third Sunday in Lent

Exodus 17:1-7
Water from the rock
Psalm 95
The rock of our salvation
Romans 5:1-11
Reconciled to God by Christ's death
John 4:5-42
The woman at the well

Reflection on Sunday

Monday
Genesis 24:1-27
Rebekah at the well
2 John 1-13
A woman reminded to abide in Christ

Tuesday
Genesis 29:1-14
Rachel at the well
1 Corinthians 10:1-5
Drink from Christ, the spiritual rock

Wednesday
Jeremiah 2:4-13
God, the living water
John 7:14-31, 37-39
Drink of Jesus, the Messiah

Daily
Psalm 81
The wicked and the righteous

FOURTH SUNDAY IN LENT

Preparation for Sunday

Thursday
1 Samuel 15:10-21
The prophet Samuel confronts the king
Ephesians 4:25-32
Called to honesty and forbearance

Friday
1 Samuel 15:22-31
The king confesses his sinful disobedience
Ephesians 5:1-7
Christ calls us to love as our obedience

Saturday
1 Samuel 15:32-34
God repents and prepares a new thing
John 1:1-9
Christ brings light into a darkened world

Daily
Psalm 23
My head anointed with oil

Fourth Sunday in Lent

1 Samuel 16:1-13
David is chosen and anointed
Psalm 23
My head anointed with oil
Ephesians 5:8-14
Live as children of light
John 9:1-41
The man born blind

Reflection on Sunday

Monday
Isaiah 59:9-19
We await God to heal our vision
Acts 9:1-20
Saul's baptism

Tuesday
Isaiah 42:14-21
God will heal the blind
Colossians 1:9-14
The inheritance of the saints in light

Wednesday
Isaiah 60:17-22
God our light
Matthew 9:27-34
Jesus heals the blind

Daily
Psalm 146:3-9
Praise to God

FIFTH SUNDAY IN LENT

Preparation for Sunday

Thursday
Ezekiel 1:1-3; 2:8—3:3
The word of God: lamentation and sweetness
Revelation 10:1-11
The word of God: bitter and sweet

Friday
Ezekiel 33:10-16
The word of God: repent and live
Revelation 11:15-19
The word of God: thanksgiving and singing

Saturday
Ezekiel 36:8-15
Blessings upon Israel
Luke 24:44-53
Jesus blesses the disciples

Daily
Psalm 130
Mercy and redemption

Fifth Sunday in Lent

Ezekiel 37:1-14
The dry bones of Israel
Psalm 130
Mercy and redemption
Romans 8:6-11
Life in the Spirit
John 11:1-45
The raising of Lazarus

Reflection on Sunday

Monday
1 Kings 17:17-24
Elijah raises the widow's son
Acts 20:7-12
Paul raises a young man

Tuesday
2 Kings 4:18-37
Elisha raises a child from death
Ephesians 2:1-10
Alive in Christ

Wednesday
Jeremiah 32:1-9, 36-41
Jeremiah buys a field
Matthew 22:23-33
God of the living

Daily
Psalm 143
Save me from death

SUNDAY OF THE PASSION
Palm Sunday

Preparation for Sunday

Thursday
1 Samuel 16:11-13
Samuel anoints David
Philippians 1:1-11
Follow Christ's righteousness

Friday
Job 13:13-19
A servant keeps silence
Philippians 1:21-30
Seeing Christ in this life

Saturday
Lamentations 3:55-66
A cry for help
Matthew 21:1-11
God's servant comes to Jerusalem

Daily
Psalm 31:9-16
I commit my spirit

Sixth Sunday in Lent

Psalm 118:1-2, 19-29
The passover praise psalm
Matthew 21:1-11
Jesus enters Jerusalem

Isaiah 50:4-9a
The servant submits to suffering
Psalm 31:9-16
I commit my spirit
Philippians 2:5-11
Death on a cross
Matthew 26:14—27:66
The passion and death of Jesus

Monday in Holy Week
Isaiah 42:1-9
The servant brings forth justice
Psalm 36:5-11
Refuge under the shadow of your wings
Hebrews 9:11-15
The blood of Christ redeems for eternal life
John 12:1-11
Mary of Bethany anoints Jesus

Tuesday in Holy Week
Isaiah 49:1-7
The servant brings salvation to earth's ends
Psalm 71:1-14
From my mother's womb you are my strength
1 Corinthians 1:18-31
The cross reveals God's power and wisdom
John 12:20-36
Jesus speaks of his death

Wednesday in Holy Week
Isaiah 50:4-9a
The servant is vindicated by God
Psalm 70
Be pleased, O God, to deliver me
Hebrews 12:1-3
Look to Jesus, who endured the cross
John 13:21-32
Jesus foretells his betrayal

THE THREE DAYS

Maundy Thursday
Exodus 12:1-4 [5-10] 11-14
The passover of the Lord
Psalm 116:1-2, 12-19
The cup of salvation
1 Corinthians 11:23-26
Proclaim the Lord's death
John 13:1-17, 31b-35
The service of Christ: footwashing and meal

Good Friday
Isaiah 52:13—53:12
The suffering servant
Psalm 22
Why have you forsaken me?
Hebrews 10:16-25   *or*   Hebrews 4:14-16; 5:7-9
The way to God is opened   *The merciful high priest*
John 18:1—19:42
The passion and death of Jesus

Holy Saturday *(at services other than the Vigil of Easter)*
Job 14:1-14   *or*   Lamentations 3:1-9, 19-24
Hope for a tree   *I will hope in the Lord*
Psalm 31:1-4, 15-16
Take me out of the net
1 Peter 4:1-8
The gospel proclaimed even to the dead
Matthew 27:57-66   *or*   John 19:38-42
The burial of Jesus   *The burial of Jesus*

Resurrection of Our Lord, Vigil of Easter

See The Church's Year, *Renewing Worship, vol. 8, for a complete list of readings and responses for the Vigil of Easter.*

Resurrection of Our Lord, Easter Day

Acts 10:34-43	*or*	Jeremiah 31:1-6
God raised Jesus on the third day		*Joy at God's people restored*
Psalm 118:1-2, 14-24		
On this day God has acted		
Colossians 3:1-4	*or*	Acts 10:34-43
Raised with Christ		*God raised Jesus on the third day*
John 20:1-18	*or*	Matthew 28:1-10
Seeing the risen Christ		*Proclaim the resurrection*

Reflection on Sunday

Monday
Exodus 14:10-31; 15:20-21
Israel crosses over the sea
Colossians 3:5-11
The new life in Christ

Tuesday
Exodus 15:1-18
The song of the sea
Colossians 3:12-17
The new life in Christ

Wednesday
Joshua 3:1-17
Israel crosses into the promised land
Matthew 28:1-10
Proclaim the resurrection

Daily
Psalm 118:1-2, 14-24
On this day God has acted

EASTER

SECOND SUNDAY OF EASTER

Preparation for Sunday

Thursday
Song of Solomon 2:8-15
The song of lovers in the garden
Colossians 4:2-5
The new life in Christ

Friday
Song of Solomon 5:9—6:3
The beloved in the garden
1 Corinthians 15:1-11
Witnesses to the risen Christ

Saturday
Song of Solomon 7:6-7
Love is strong as death
John 20:11-20
The witness of Mary Magdalene

Daily
Psalm 16
Fullness of joy

Second Sunday of Easter

Acts 2:14a, 22-32
God fulfills the promise to David
Psalm 16
Fullness of joy
1 Peter 1:3-9
New birth to a living hope
John 20:19-31
Beholding the wounds of the risen Christ

Reflection on Sunday

Monday
Judges 6:36-40
Gideon and the fleece
1 Corinthians 15:12-20
Paul teaches the resurrection

Tuesday
Jonah 1:1-17
Jonah saved from the sea
1 Corinthians 15:19-28
Paul teaches the resurrection

Wednesday
Jonah 2:1-10
Jonah's praise for deliverance
Matthew 12:38-42
Jesus speaks of the sign of Jonah

Daily
Psalm 114
God saves through water

THIRD SUNDAY OF EASTER

Preparation for Sunday

Thursday
Isaiah 25:1-5
Praise for deliverance
1 Peter 1:8b-12
The promised salvation comes

Friday
Isaiah 26:1-4
God sets up victory like bulwarks
1 Peter 1:13-16
A holy life

Saturday
Isaiah 25:6-9
The feast for all peoples
Luke 14:12-14
Welcome those in need to your table

Daily
Psalm 116:1-4, 12-19
I will call upon God

Third Sunday of Easter

> Acts 2:14a, 36-41
> *Receiving God's promise through baptism*
> Psalm 116:1-4, 12-19
> *I will call upon God*
> 1 Peter 1:17-23
> *Born anew*
> Luke 24:13-35
> *Eating with the risen Christ*

Reflection on Sunday

Monday
Genesis 18:1-14
Abraham and Sarah eat with God
1 Peter 1:23-25
The word of God endures

Tuesday
Proverbs 8:32—9:6
Wisdom serves a meal
1 Peter 2:1-2
Long for the pure spiritual milk

Wednesday
Exodus 24:1-11
Moses and the elders eat with God
John 21:1-14
The risen Christ eats with the disciples

Daily
Psalm 134
Praise God day and night

FOURTH SUNDAY OF EASTER

Preparation for Sunday

Thursday
Exodus 2:15b-25
Moses the shepherd
1 Peter 2:9-12
Living as God's people

Friday
Exodus 3:16-22; 4:18-20
Moses the shepherd of Israel
1 Peter 2:13-17
Living honorably in the world

Saturday
Ezekiel 34:1-16
God gathers the scattered flock
Luke 15:1-7
Parable of the lost sheep

Daily
Psalm 23
God our shepherd

Fourth Sunday of Easter

Acts 2:42-47
The believers' common life
Psalm 23
God our shepherd
1 Peter 2:19-25
Follow the shepherd, even in suffering
John 10:1-10
Christ the shepherd

Reflection on Sunday

Monday
Ezekiel 34:17-23
God the true shepherd
1 Peter 5:1-5
Tend the flock of God

Tuesday
Ezekiel 34:23-31
God provides perfect pasture
Hebrews 13:20-21
God's blessing through Christ the shepherd

Wednesday
Jeremiah 23:1-8
God will gather the flock
Matthew 20:17-28
Jesus came to serve

Daily
Psalm 100
We are the sheep of God's pasture

FIFTH SUNDAY OF EASTER

Preparation for Sunday

Thursday
Genesis 12:1-3
Call of Abram
Acts 7:1-16
Stephen addresses the council

Friday
Exodus 3:1-12
Moses at the burning bush
Acts 7:17-50
Stephen addresses the council

Saturday
Jeremiah 26:20-24
A prophet is persecuted
John 8:48-59
Jesus the greater prophet

Daily
Psalm 31:1-5, 15-16
I commend my spirit

Fifth Sunday of Easter

> Acts 7:55-60
> *Martyrdom of Stephen*
> Psalm 31:1-5, 15-16
> *I commend my spirit*
> 1 Peter 2:2-10
> *God's chosen people*
> John 14:1-14
> *Christ the way, truth, life*

Reflection on Sunday

Monday
Exodus 13:17-22
God leads the way
Acts 6:8-15
Stephen is arrested

Tuesday
Proverbs 3:5-12
God the truth and life
Acts 7:44-54
Stephen is martyred

Wednesday
Proverbs 3:13-18
God the truth and life
John 8:31-38
Jesus, the truth of God

Daily
Psalm 102:1-17
Prayer for deliverance

SIXTH SUNDAY OF EASTER

Preparation for Sunday

Thursday
Genesis 6:5-22
Command to Noah
Acts 27:1-12
Paul sails for Rome

Friday
Genesis 7:1-24
The great flood
Acts 27:13-38
Paul survives shipwreck

Saturday
Genesis 8:13-19
The flood subsides
John 14:27-29
Peace I leave with you

Daily
Psalm 66:8-20
Be joyful in God, all you lands

Sixth Sunday of Easter

Acts 17:22-31
Paul's message to the Athenians
Psalm 66:8-20
Be joyful in God, all you lands
1 Peter 3:13-22
The days of Noah, a sign of baptism
John 14:15-21
Christ our advocate

Reflection on Sunday

Monday
Genesis 9:8-17
Sign of the covenant
Acts 27:39-44
Paul and companions come safely to land

Tuesday
Deuteronomy 5:22-33
Moses delivers God's commandments
1 Peter 3:8-12
Seek peace and pursue it

Wednesday
Deuteronomy 31:1-13
Moses promises God's presence
John 16:16-24
A little while, and you shall see

Daily
Psalm 93
God reigns above the floods

SEVENTH SUNDAY OF EASTER

Thursday, Ascension of Our Lord

Acts 1:1-11
Jesus sends the apostles
Psalm 47   *or*   Psalm 93
God has gone up with a shout   *Praise to God who reigns*
Ephesians 1:15-23
Seeing the risen and ascended Christ
Luke 24:44-53
Christ present in all times and places

Preparation for Sunday

Friday   **Daily**
2 Kings 2:1-12   Psalm 93
Elijah ascends in a chariot of fire   *Praise to God who reigns*
Ephesians 2:1-7
Seated in the heavenly places with Christ

Saturday
2 Kings 2:13-15
The spirit rests on Elisha
John 8:21-30
Jesus speaks of going to the Father

Seventh Sunday of Easter

Acts 1:6-14
Jesus' companions at prayer
Psalm 68:1-10, 32-35
Sing to God
1 Peter 4:12-14; 5:6-11
God sustains those who suffer
John 17:1-11
Christ's prayer for his disciples

Reflection on Sunday

Monday
Leviticus 9:1-11, 22-24
The high priest Aaron offers sacrifice
1 Peter 4:1-6
Live by the will of God

Tuesday
Numbers 16:41-50
The high priest Aaron makes atonement
1 Peter 4:7-11
Be good stewards of grace

Wednesday
1 Kings 8:54-65
Solomon offers sacrifice
John 3:31-36
The Son and the Father

Daily
Psalm 99
Priests and people praise God

DAY OF PENTECOST

Preparation for Sunday

Thursday
Exodus 19:1-9
The covenant at Sinai
Acts 2:1-11
A covenant with the Spirit

Friday
Exodus 19:16-25
Moses and Aaron meet the LORD
Romans 8:14-17
Led by the Spirit of God

Saturday
Exodus 20:1-21
Moses brings the Ten Words to Israel
Matthew 5:1-11
Jesus brings blessings to his community

Daily
Psalm 33:12-22
Our help and our shield

Day of Pentecost

Acts 2:1-21
Filled with the Spirit
Psalm 104:24-34, 35b
Renewing the face of the earth
1 Corinthians 12:3b-13
Varieties of gifts, the same Spirit
John 20:19-23
The Spirit poured out

or

Numbers 11:24-30
The spirit rests on Israel's leaders

Acts 2:1-21
Filled with the Spirit

Reflection on Sunday

Monday
Joel 2:18-29
God promises the Spirit
Romans 8:18-24
We have the first fruits of the Spirit

Tuesday
Ezekiel 34:7-8, 21-29
God promises the Spirit
Romans 8:26-27
Praying in the Spirit

Wednesday
Numbers 11:24-30
The spirit rests on Israel's elders
John 7:37-39
Jesus, the true living water

Daily
Psalm 104:24-34, 35b
Renewing the face of the earth

RENEWING ✦ WORSHIP

Service Music

R 401   **Joyous Light of glory**
Light hymn

Continue on next page ▸

Text: *Worship & Praise,* based on Greek hymn
Music: Ralph C. Sappington
Text and music © 1999 Augsburg Fortress. All rights reserved.

R 402 O radiant Light, O Sun divine
Light hymn

1. O radiant Light, O Sun divine of God the Father's deathless face, O image of the Light sublime that fills the heav'nly dwelling place:
2. O Son of God, the source of life, praise is your due by night and day. Our happy lips must raise the strain of your esteemed and splendid name.
3. Lord Jesus Christ, as daylight fades, as shine the lights of eventide, we praise the Father with the Son, the Spirit blest, and with them one. Amen.

Text: William G. Storey, based on Greek hymn
Music: JESU DULCIS MEMORIA plainsong, mode 1; arr. Theodore Marier, *ICEL Resource Collection*
Text © William G. Storey, admin. GIA Publications, Inc.. All rights reserved.
You must contact GIA Publications at 800/GIA-1358 for permission to reproduce this text.

R 403 O gracious Light
Light hymn

Text: Greek hymn, tr. *Book of Common Prayer*
Music: Ronald Arnatt
Music © 1985 Church Pension Fund
You must contact Church Publishing Corp. at 800/223-6602 for permission to reproduce this music.

R 404 O laughing Light
Light hymn

1 O laughing Light, O First-born of creation, radiance of glory, light from light begotten, God self-revealing, holy, bright, and blessed: you shine upon us.

2 Day's light is fragile; your light is eternal. We look to you, our light within the shadow. We sing to you, Creator, Christ, and Spirit; you shine before us.

3 Light of the world, O Jesus, you are worthy! Giver of life and Child of God, we praise you! Hear as the universe proclaims your glory! You shine among us.

Text: Sylvia G. Dunstan, based on Greek hymn
Music: Richard W. Dirksen
Text © 1991 GIA Publications, Inc. All rights reserved.
Music © 1984 Washington National Cathedral
You must contact the copyright administrators for permission to reproduce this selection.

R 405 **Let my prayer rise before you**
Psalm 141

Text: Psalm 141, tr. *Book of Common Prayer*
Music: David Schack
Music © 1978 *Lutheran Book of Worship,* admin. Augsburg Fortress. All rights reserved.

R 406 **Let my prayer rise up**
Psalm 141

118 DAILY PRAYER

120　DAILY PRAYER

Text: Marty Haugen, based on Psalm 141
Music: Marty Haugen
Text and music © 1990 GIA Publications, Inc. All rights reserved.
You must contact GIA Publications at 800/GIA-1358 for permission to reproduce this selection.

R 407 Suba a ti mi oración
Let my prayer rise before you

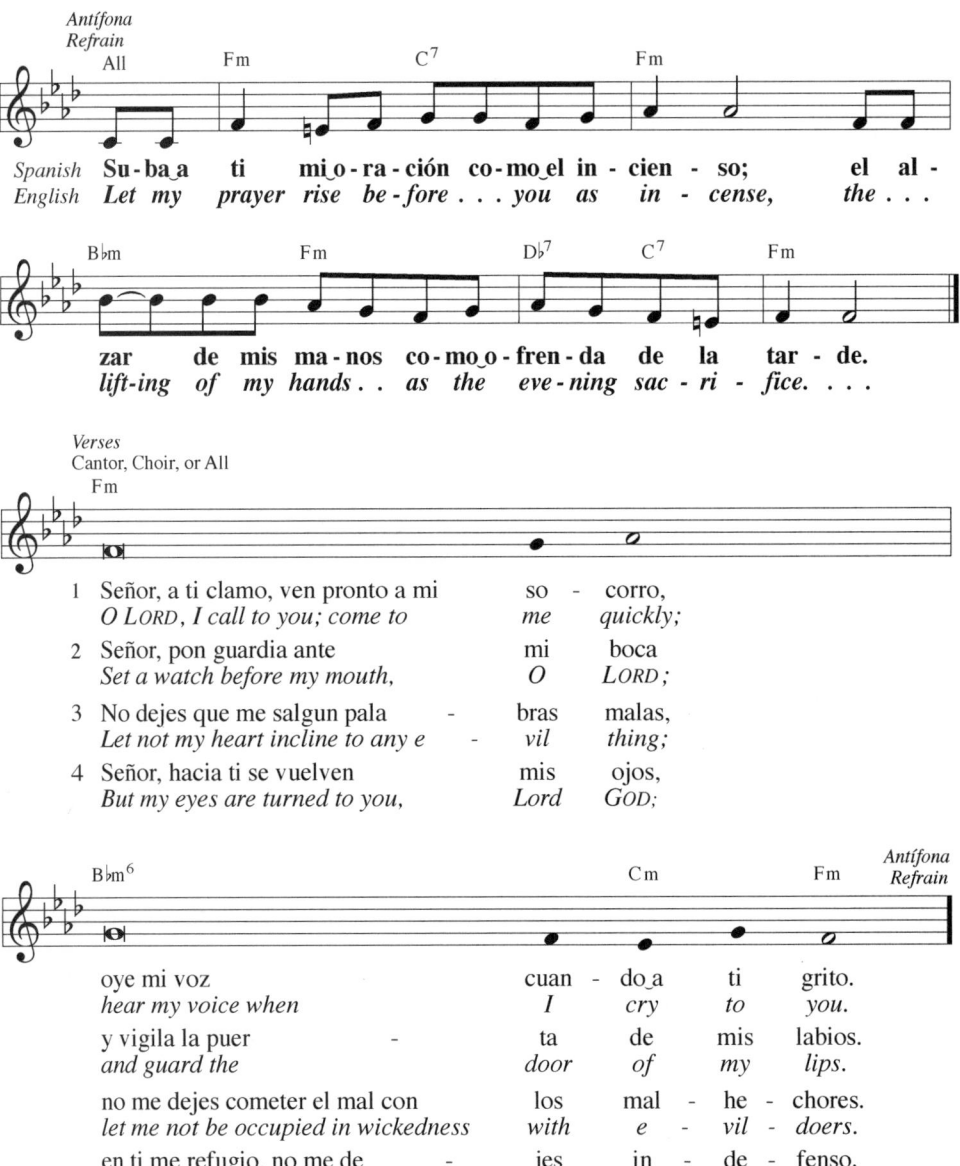

1. Señor, a ti clamo, ven pronto a mi socorro,
   O LORD, I call to you; come to me quickly;
2. Señor, pon guardia ante mi boca
   Set a watch before my mouth, O LORD;
3. No dejes que me salgun palabras malas,
   Let not my heart incline to any evil thing;
4. Señor, hacia ti se vuelven mis ojos,
   But my eyes are turned to you, Lord GOD;

oye mi voz cuando a ti grito.
hear my voice when I cry to you.
y vigila la puerta de mis labios.
and guard the door of my lips.
no me dejes cometer el mal con los malhechores.
let me not be occupied in wickedness with evildoers.
en ti me refugio, no me dejes indefenso.
in you I take refuge; strip me not of my life.

Text: Psalm 141; English *Book of Common Prayer;* Spanish *Libro de Liturgia y Cántico*
Music: Gerhard Cartford
Music © 1998 Augsburg Fortress. All rights reserved.

R 408 **Let my prayer arise before you**
Psalm 141

1. O LORD, I call to you;
   come | to me quickly;*
   hear my voice when I | cry to you.

2. Let my prayer be set forth
   in your | sight as incense,*
   the lifting up of my hands
   as the evening | sacrifice. *Refrain*

3. Set a watch before my | mouth, O LORD,*
   and guard the door | of my lips.

4. Let not my heart incline
   to any | evil thing;*
   let me not be occupied
   in wickedness with | evildoers. *Refrain*

5. But my eyes are turned to | you,
   Lord GOD;*
   in you I take refuge;
   strip me | not of my life. *Refrain*

Text: Psalm 141, tr. *Book of Common Prayer*
Music: Leon C. Roberts
Music © 1999 Augsburg Fortress. All rights reserved.

R 409 **Let my prayer rise up as incense**
Psalm 141

126 DAILY PRAYER

Text: Psalm 141, tr. *Book of Common Prayer*
Music: David Cherwien
Music © 2001 Augsburg Fortress. All rights reserved.

R 410 **My soul proclaims the greatness of the Lord**
Magnificat

Text: Luke 1:47-55, English Language Liturgical Consultation version
Music: Robert Moore
Text © 1988 English Language Liturgical Consultation
Music © 2004 Augsburg Fortress. All rights reserved.

R 411 My soul proclaims the greatness of the Lord
Magnificat

Continue on next page ▶

SERVICE MUSIC   133

Text: Luke 1:47-55, English Language Liturgical Consultation version
Music: Russell Schulz-Widmar
Text © 1988 English Language Liturgical Consultation
Music © 2004 Augsburg Fortress. All rights reserved.

R 412 My soul does magnify the Lord
Magnificat

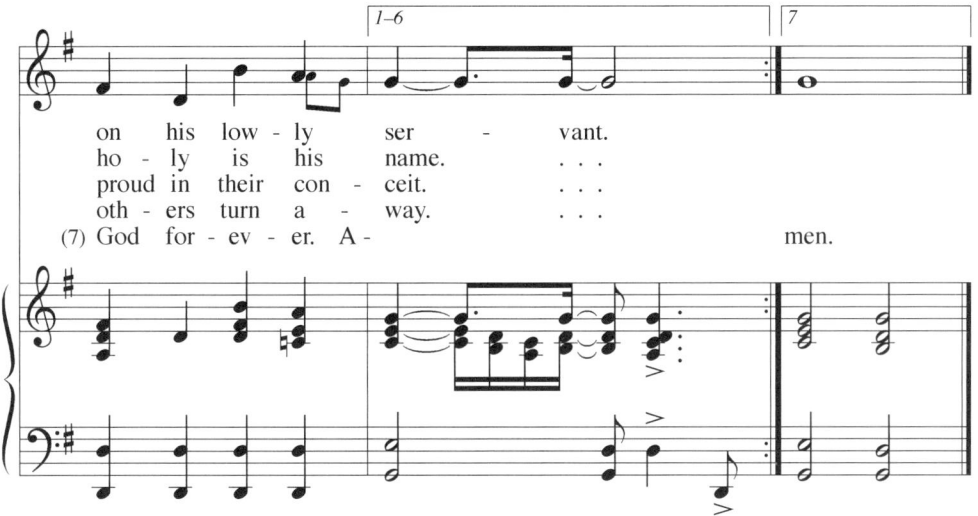

5 He comes to all who seek his love,
   for he remembers the promise
   that he had made to Abraham
      and to the children of God.

6 All glory be to God on high,
   and to his Son, God the Savior,
   and to the Spirit of life and truth
      that burns within our hearts.

7 Just as it was, it is today,
   and it shall last through all tomorrows,
   and so my soul magnifies the Lord;
      praise God forever. Amen.

Text: Grayson Warren Brown, based on Luke 1:47-55
Music: Grayson Warren Brown
Text and music © 1992 Grayson Warren Brown. Published by OCP Publications, 5536 NE Hassalo, Portland, OR 97213.
You must contact OCP Publications at 800/548-8749 for permission to reproduce this selection.

R 413 Mary's Salidummay
Magnificat

1. My soul magnifies the Lord, and in God my heart exults: "Salidum salidumay, in sinalidumiway. Ay ay Salidummay."
2. Favored look he cast on me, shadowed me so tenderly, generations then will see God works silently. Ay ay Salidummay.
3. To God-fearing souls he goes, on them mercy he bestows; with the strength of his right arm scatters all the proud who swarm. Ay ay Salidummay.
4. Those enthroned he will bring down, and the lowly he will crown; hungry ones he'll fill with cheer, but the rich his day will fear. Ay ay Salidummay.
5. So the promise from of old comes to life, has not gone cold; promise made to Abraham bears its fruit, the kingdom come. Ay ay Salidummay.

Text: Henry W. Kiley, based on Luke 1:47-55
Music: Henry W. Kiley
Text and music © Henry W. Kiley, admin. Christian Conference of Asia
You must contact Christian Conference of Asia at 852/2691-1068 for permission to reproduce this selection.

This hymn from the Philippines is best sung unaccompanied, or possibly with a light melody instrument and finger cymbals or a triangle. Approximate pronunciation: sah-lee-doom sah-lee-doo-may, in see-nah-lee-doo-mee-way, ay ay sah-lee-doo-may. The meaning of *Salidummay* has long been forgotten, but Christians have adapted the word to express the mood of joy.

R 414 In peace, let us pray
Litany

Additional petitions may be sung by the leader using the above tone. The response follows each petition, with the assembly overlapping the leader on the word "Lord." At the conclusion of the litany:

. . . through Jesus Christ our Lord.

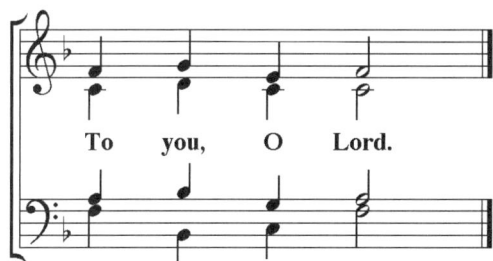

Music: Byzantine traditional

R 415 Kyrie eleison
Litany

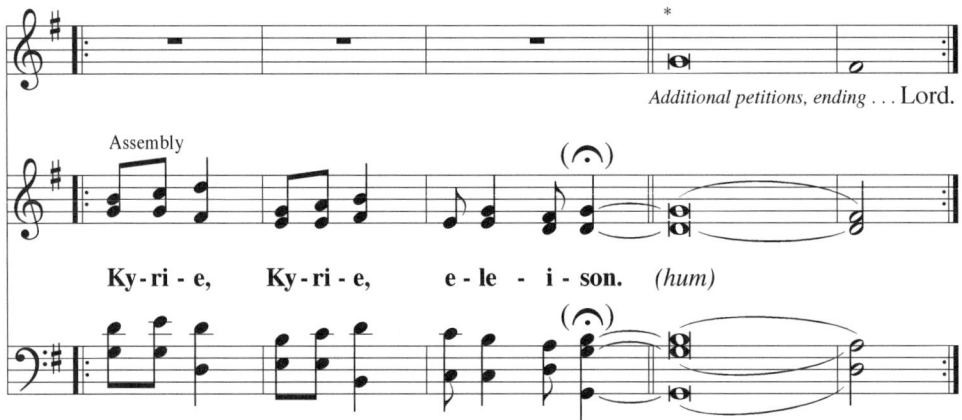

* Omit the final two measures after the last petition and response.

Additional petitions may be sung by the leader using the above tone. The response follows each petition and is also sung at the conclusion of the litany.

Music: Jacques Berthier
Music © 1979 Les Presses de Taizé, admin. GIA Publications, Inc., exclusive agent. All rights reserved.
You must contact GIA Publications at 800/GIA-1358 for permission to reproduce this selection.

R 416 God of mercy, hold us in love
Litany

5 For all of your servants who live out your gospel:
   God of mercy, hold us in love.

6 For all those who govern, that justice might guide them:
   God of mercy, hold us in love.

7 For all those who labor in service to others:
   God of mercy, hold us in love.

8 Grant weather that nourishes all creation:
   God of mercy, hold us in love.

9 Keep watch on our loved ones and keep us from danger:
   God of mercy, hold us in love.

10 For all the belovèd who rest in your mercy:
   God of mercy, hold us in love.

Text and music: Marty Haugen
Text and music © 1990 GIA Publications, Inc. All rights reserved.
You must contact GIA Publications at 800/GIA-1358 for permission to reproduce this selection.

R 417 Come, let us sing to the Lord
Venite

144 DAILY PRAYER

Text: Psalm 95:1-7a, *Book of Common Prayer*, alt.
Music: Carolyn Jennings
Text and music © 2004 Augsburg Fortress. All rights reserved.

R 418 Come, let us sing to the Lord
Venite

This psalm may be performed in unison throughout or as follows:

Verse 1: sung by cantor

Verse 2: sung by choir trebles, TB, or unison

Verse 3: sung by choir in unison

Verse 4: sung by whole congregation

Text: Psalm 95:1-7, New Revised Standard Version Bible, alt.
Music: Jack Noble White
Text © 1989 Division of Christian Education of the National Council of Churches of Christ in the United States of America
Music © 1971 Walton Music Corp.
You must contact Walton Music Corp. at 304/563-1844 for permission to reproduce this music.

R 419 Oh, come, let us sing
Venite

Text: *Worship & Praise,* based on Psalm 95:1-7a
Music: Ben Houge
Text and music © 1999 Augsburg Fortress. All rights reserved.

R 420 Come, ring out your joy to the Lord
Venite

154 DAILY PRAYER

1 Come, let us sing | to the LORD;*
   let us shout for joy to the rock of | our salvation.
2 Let us come before God's presence | with thanksgiving*
   and raise a loud shout to the | LORD with psalms.
3 For you, LORD, | are a great God,*
   and a great ruler a- | bove all gods. *Refrain*

4 In your hand are the caverns | of the earth;*
   the heights of the hills are | also yours.
5 The sea is yours, | for you made it;*
   and your hands have molded | the dry land.
6 Come, let us worship | and bow down;*
   let us kneel before the | LORD our maker.
7 For the LORD | is our God,
   and we are the people of God's pasture
   and the sheep | of God's hand. *Refrain*

Text: Psalm 95:1-7a, *Book of Common Prayer*, alt.
Music: Rawn Harbor
Text © 2004 Augsburg Fortress. All rights reserved.
Music © 1999 Augsburg Fortress. All rights reserved.

R 421 Blessed are you, Lord
Benedictus

Text: Luke 1:68-79, English Language Liturgical Consultation version
Music: Mark Mummert
Text © 1988 English Language Liturgical Consultation
Music © 2004 Augsburg Fortress. All rights reserved.

R 422 **Blessed are you, Lord**
Benedictus

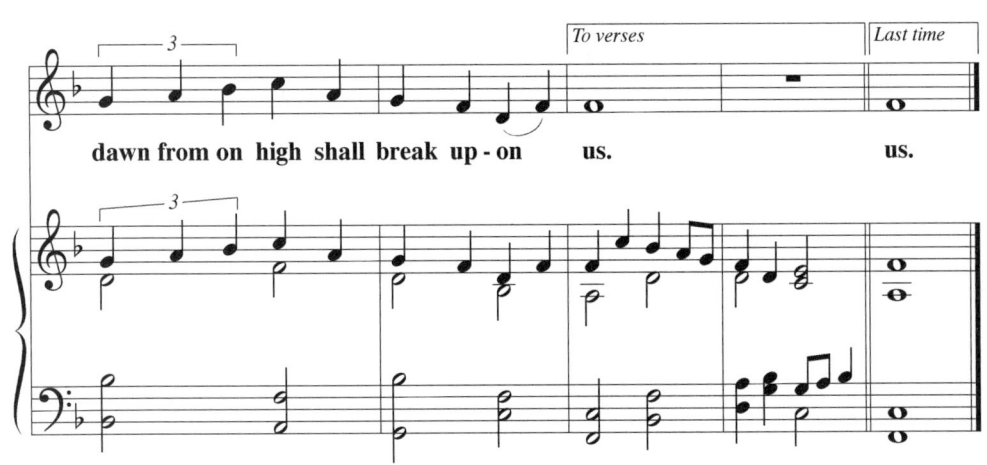

164 DAILY PRAYER

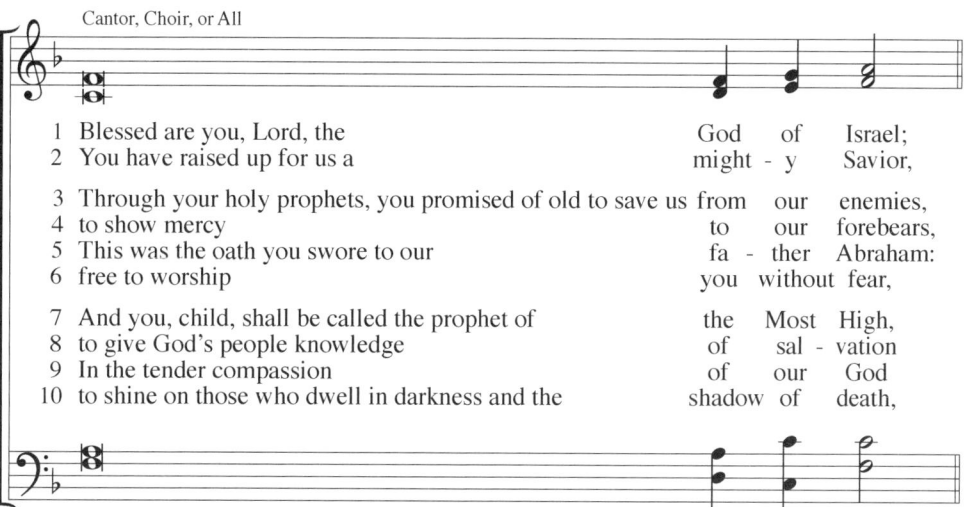
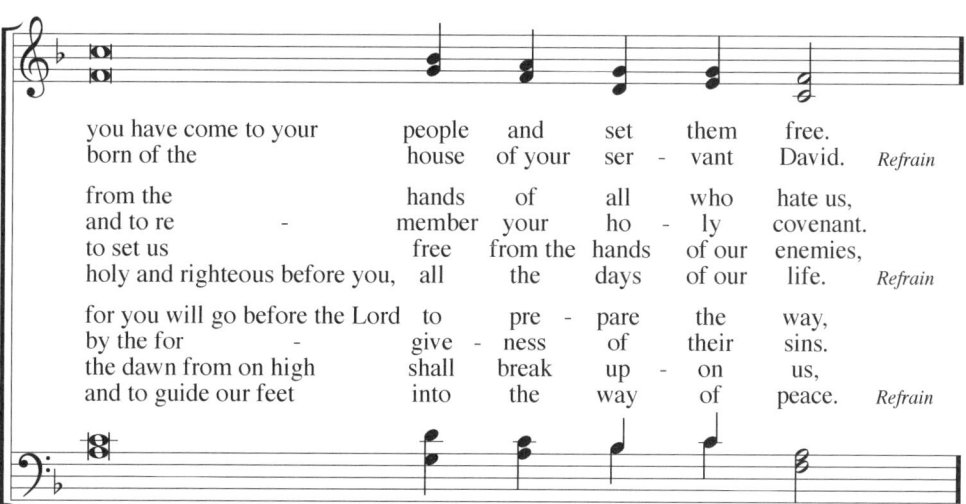

Text: Luke 1:68-79, English Language Liturgical Consultation version
Music: Mark Mummert
Text © 1988 English Language Liturgical Consultation
Music © 2004 Augsburg Fortress. All rights reserved.

R 423 Blessed are you, Lord
Benedictus

SERVICE MUSIC 169

Text: Luke 1:68-79, English Language Liturgical Consultation version
Music: Anne Krentz Organ
Text © 1988 English Language Liturgical Consultation
Music © 2004 Augsburg Fortress. All rights reserved.

R 424 Blessed be the God of Israel
Benedictus

1 Blessed be the God of Israel, who comes to set us free,
  who visits and redeems us, and grants us liberty.
  The prophets spoke of mercy, of freedom and release;
  God shall fulfill the promise to bring our people peace.

2 Now from the house of David a child of grace has come,
  a Savior who will lead us to our eternal home.
  Before him goes the herald, forerunner in the way,
  the prophet of salvation, the harbinger of day.

3 On all by death imprisoned the sun begins to rise,
  the dawning of forgiveness upon the sinner's eyes,
  to guide the feet of pilgrims along the paths of peace;
  oh, bless our God and Savior with songs that never cease!

Text: Michael Perry, based on Luke 1:68-79
Music: MERLE'S TUNE Hal H. Hopson
Text © 1973 *Jubilate Hymns,* admin. Hope Publishing Company
Music © 1983 Hope Publishing Company
You must contact Hope Publishing Company at 800/323-1049 for permission to reproduce this selection.

SERVICE MUSIC   171

R 425 **We praise you, O God**
Te Deum

Text: Latin hymn, English Language Liturgical Consultation version
Music: Robert Buckley Farlee
Text © 1988 English Language Liturgical Consultation
Music © 2001 Robert Buckley Farlee, admin. Augsburg Fortress. All rights reserved.

R 426 We praise you, O God
Te Deum

1 We praise you, O God, we acclaim you as Lord;
  all creation worships you, the Father everlasting.
2 To you all angels, all the pow'rs of heav'n,
  the cherubim and seraphim, sing in endless praise.
3 Holy, holy, holy Lord, God of pow'r and might,
  heaven and earth are full of your glory.
4 The glorious company of apostles praise . . . you.
  The noble fellowship of prophets praise . . . you.
5 The white-robed army of martyrs praise . . . you.
  Throughout the world the holy church acclaims you:
6 Father, of majesty unbounded; your true and only Son, worthy of all praise;
  the Holy Spirit, advocate and guide.
7 You, Christ, are the king of glory,
  the eternal Son of the Father.

178   DAILY PRAYER

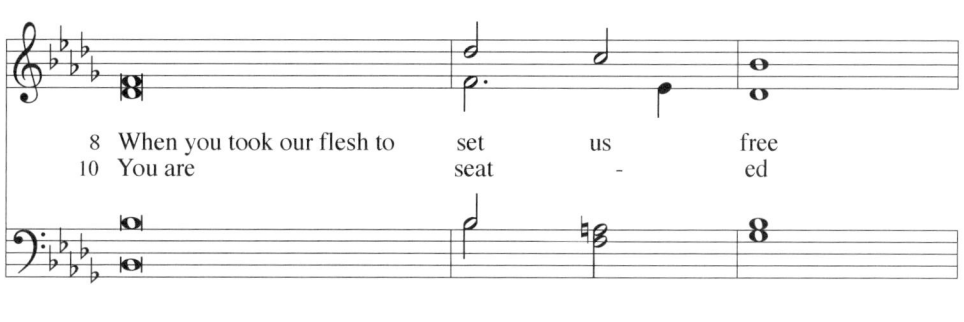
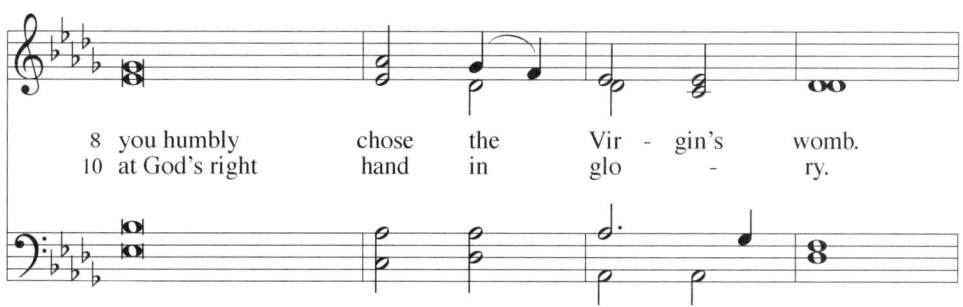
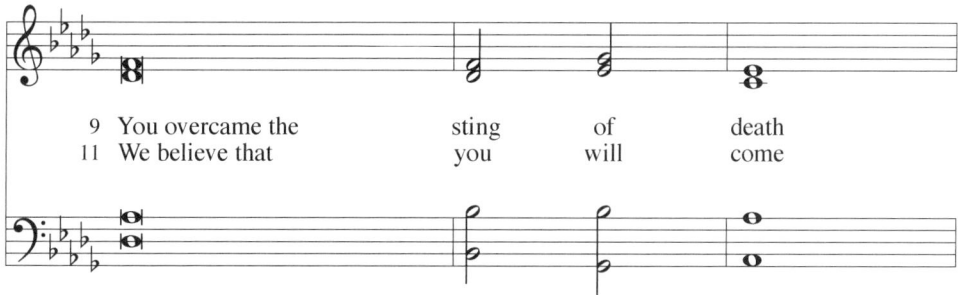

SERVICE MUSIC

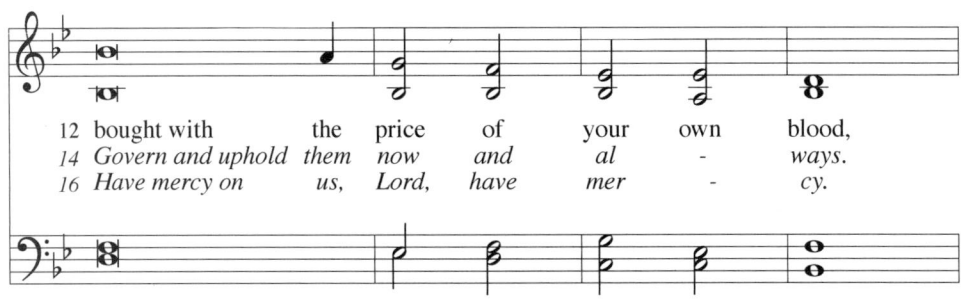
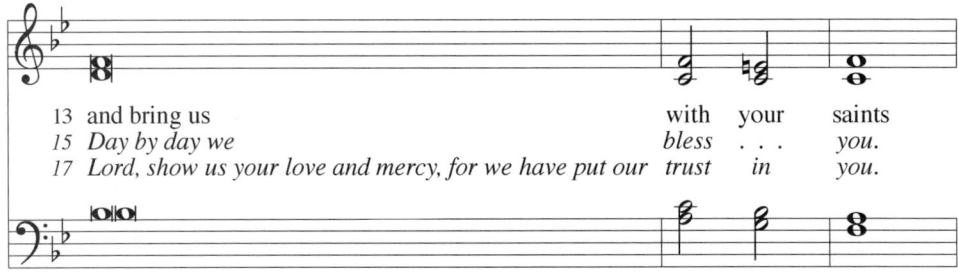
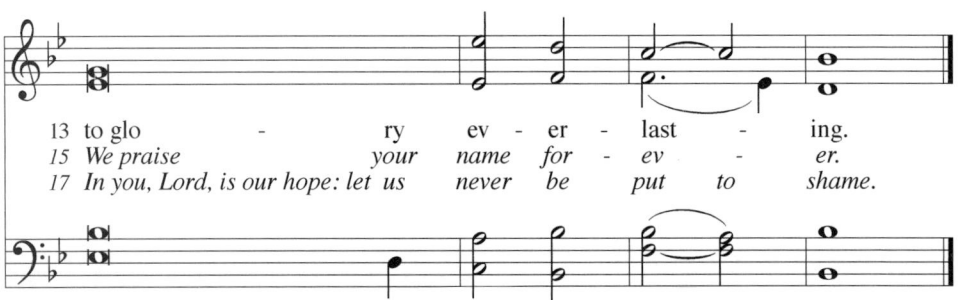

The versicles and responses in italics are not part of the original but were appended at an early date.

Text: Latin hymn, English Language Liturgical Consultation version
Music: H. Lawes and R. Cooke
Text © 1988 English Language Liturgical Consultation

Acknowledgments

Daily Prayer editorial team: Robert Hawkins, Diane Jacobson, Dirk Lange, E. Louise Williams; Michael Burk, Cheryl Dieter, Martin A. Seltz (Renewing Worship project management staff).

Daily Prayer development panel: Susan Briehl, Lorraine Brugh, Nora Frost, Carol Hendrix, Ralph Klein, Gordon Lathrop, Carlos Messerli, George Murphy, Philip Pfatteicher, Robert Rimbo, Jakob Rinderknecht, Ronald Roschke, Thomas Schattauer, May Schwarz, Joyce Ann Zimmermann.

Liturgical Music editorial team: Kevin Anderson, Teresa Bowers, Lorraine Brugh, David Cherwien, Thomas Pavlechko, Scott Weidler; Michael Burk, Cheryl Dieter, Martin A. Seltz (Renewing Worship project management staff).

Design and production: Jessica Hillstrom, Mark Weiler, production; Carolyn Porter of The Kantor Group, Inc., book design; Nicholas Markell, logo design.

The material on pages i—192 is covered by the copyright of this book. Unless otherwise noted, the material has been prepared by the editorial team. Material from the sources listed here is gratefully acknowledged and is used by permission. Every effort has been made to identify the copyright administrators for copyrighted texts and music. The publisher regrets any oversight that may have occurred and will make proper acknowledgment in future editions if correct information is brought to the publisher's attention.

Scripture translation quotations (original and emended), unless otherwise noted, are from the New Revised Standard Version Bible © 1989 Division of Christian Education of the National Council of Churches of Christ in the United States of America. Used by permission.

Between Sundays: Daily Bible Readings Based on the Revised Common Lectionary, © 1997 Augsburg Fortress: selected citations in daily lectionary, 67-99

The Book of Common Prayer (1979) of The Episcopal Church: psalm examples, 30–38

Book of Common Worship, © 1993 Westminster John Knox Press: morning prayer, prayers, 26

"Daily Readings for the Revised Common Lectionary," unpublished, © 2004 Consultation on Common Texts, admin. Augsburg Fortress: daily lectionary scripture citations, 67–99

Holy Baptism and Related Rites, Renewing Worship, vol. 3, © 2002 admin. Augsburg Fortress: morning prayer, conclusion of remembrance of baptism, 13

Lutheran Book of Worship, © 1978 Lutheran Church in America, The American Lutheran Church, The Evangelical Lutheran Church of Canada, and the Lutheran Church–Missouri Synod, admin. Augsburg Fortress: evening prayer, morning prayer, night prayer, supplemental materials, 5–27 (selected texts)

Praying Together, © 1998 English Language Liturgical Consultation: texts of "Blessed are you, Lord" (Benedictus), "My soul proclaims the greatness of the Lord" (Magnificat), "Our Father in heaven"

Psalms class, Luther Seminary, St. Paul, Diane Jacobson, professor: prayer of lament, 36-38

The Revised Common Lectionary, © 1992 Consultation on Common Texts, admin. Augsburg Fortress: scripture citations for Sundays and festivals, 67–99

Worship resources project of the ELCA Alliance for Faith, Science, and Technology: thanksgiving for light C, 25

Service music credits appear with the music in the Service Music section.

Indexes

TEXT AND MUSIC SOURCES

Arnatt, Ronald R403
Berthier, Jacques R415
Book of Common Prayer R403, R405, R407, R408, R409, R417, R420
Brown, Grayson Warren R412
Byzantine traditional R414
Cartford, Gerhard R407
Cherwien, David R409
Cooke, R. R426
Dirksen, Richard W. R404
Dunstan, Sylvia G. R404
English Language Liturgical Consultation R410, R411, R421, R422, R423, R425, R426
Farlee, Robert Buckley R425
Greek hymn R403
Greek hymn, based on R401, R402, R404
Harbor, Rawn R420
Haugen, Marty R406, R416
Hopson, Hal H. R424
Houge, Ben R419
Jennings, Carolyn R417
Kiley, Henry W. R413
Latin hymn R425, R426
Lawes, H. R426

Libro de Liturgia y Cántico R407
Luke 1:47-55 R410, R411
Luke 1:47-55, based on R412, R413
Luke 1:68-79 R421, R422, R423
Luke 1:68-79, based on R424
Marier, Theodore R402
Moore, Robert R410
Mummert, Mark R421, R422
Organ, Anne Krentz R423
Perry, Michael R424
Plainsong, mode 1 R402
Psalm 141 R405, R407, R408, R409
Psalm 141, based on R406
Psalm 95:1-7a R417, R420
Psalm 95:1-7a, based on R419
Psalm 95:1-7 R418
Roberts, Leon C. R408
Sappington, Ralph C. R401
Schack, David R405
Schulz-Widmar, Russell R411
Storey, William G. R402
White, Jack Noble R418
Worship & Praise R401, R419

TITLES AND FIRST LINES

Benedictus R421, R422, R423, R424
Blessed are you, Lord R421, R422, R423
Blessed be the God of Israel R424
Come, let us sing to the Lord R417, R418
Come, ring out your joy to the Lord R420
God of mercy, hold us in love R416
In peace, in peace, we pray to you R416
In peace, let us pray R414, R415
In the tender compassion of our God R421, R422
Joyous Light of glory R401
Kyrie eleison R415
Let my prayer arise before you R408
Let my prayer rise before you R405, R407
Let my prayer rise up R406
Let my prayer rise up as incense R409
Light hymn R401, R402, R403, R404

Litany R414, R415, R416
Magnificat R410, R411, R412, R413
Mary's Salidummay R413
My soul does magnify the Lord R412
My soul magnifies the Lord R413
My soul proclaims the greatness of the Lord R410, R411
O gracious Light R403
O laughing Light R404
O radiant Light, O Sun divine R402
Oh, come, let us sing R419
Psalm 141 R405, R406, R407, R408, R409
Suba a ti mi oración R407
Te Deum R425, R426
Venite R417, R418, R419, R420
We praise you, O God R425, R426

Evaluation

An essential goal of Renewing Worship is the use and evaluation of trial-use resources by worshiping communities and their leaders. Such feedback will help shape decisions on final resources. Included here as well as at www.renewingworship.org is a reproducible evaluation tool that can be used to evaluate the rites and music contained in *Daily Prayer*.

This evaluation form is separated into two parts, which will allow you to evaluate the rites (shape and texts of the liturgies) or the music. Be sure to include the completed last page of the evaluation with each submission.

Please use check marks to identify the material you are evaluating:

RITES (Questions 1-10) and TEXTS (Questions 1-3):

_____ Evening Prayer (rite)
_____ Morning Prayer (rite)
_____ Night Prayer (rite)
_____ Supplemental Materials (texts)
_____ Daily Prayer Examples (rites)
_____ Psalms (texts)
_____ Daily Lectionary (texts)

MUSIC (Questions 11-18):

Service music section R401–R426. Please identify the specific piece of liturgical music you are evaluating: R _____

Please indicate your agreement with the statements that follow by circling the appropriate number. If desired, add comments to support your response.

RITES

1. The rite/text is faithful to scripture and the church's tradition.

    Agree   Disagree
      1   2   3   4   5

Comments:

2. The style and language of the rite/text are accessible to our worshiping assembly.

    Agree   Disagree
      1   2   3   4   5

Comments:

3. (Daily Lectionary only) A three-year set of daily Bible readings related to the Sunday lectionary readings is a helpful resource for personal prayer and group worship in our congregation.

    Agree   Disagree
      1   2   3   4   5

Comments:

4. The rite is easy to follow and to adapt for our worshiping assembly.

    Agree   Disagree

      1   2   3   4   5

Comments:

5. The shape of the rite is a helpful guide to the flow and the flexibility of the liturgy.

    Agree   Disagree

      1   2   3   4   5

Comments:

6. Who was involved in the planning related to use of this rite?

____ Pastor(s)

____ Pastor(s) and musicians

____ Pastor(s), musicians, and other staff

____ Group of lay members with pastoral and other staff

____ Other (describe): _____

7. In what context was the rite used?

____ As a regularly scheduled service

____ Outside of a regularly scheduled service

____ Studied but not used in worship

____ Other (describe): _____

8. How many times did you use the rite prior to this evaluation? _____

9. One of the goals of Renewing Worship is to provide options that can be used in flexible ways. Which statement best describes the options provided in this rite?

_____ A sufficient number of options are provided with the rite.

_____ Too many options are provided with the rite.

_____ Too few options are provided with the rite.

10. Please note any additional comments and suggestions.

Please complete the information at the end of the evaluation form.

MUSIC

11. The text and the music are well-matched.

Agree				Disagree
1	2	3	4	5

Comments:

12. The music invites the assembly's active participation

Agree				Disagree
1	2	3	4	5

Comments:

13. The melody is appropriate for congregational singing.

Agree				Disagree
1	2	3	4	5

Comments:

14. The accompaniment provided is accessible to our music leader(s).

Agree				Disagree
1	2	3	4	5

Comments:

15. What type of accompaniment was used to support the singing of the music? (Select all that apply).

____ Organ
____ Piano/keyboard
____ Guitar(s)
____ Drum(s)
____ Orchestra (strings and/or wind instruments)
____ Band and/or praise band
____ Other (please specify): _____

16. How many times did you use the music prior to this evaluation? _____

17. In your opinion, should this music be included in (select one answer only):

____ A primary common resource
____ Secondary, supplemental materials
____ Not necessary to include

18. Please note any additional comments or suggestions about the music.

Please complete the information at the end of the evaluation form.

INFORMATION ABOUT THIS EVALUATION

Please provide the requested information and include it with each separately submitted evaluation, whether filled in on this form (or a photocopy of it) or in a letter.

ELCA Congregation ID # _____

If this response is not from an ELCA congregation or you do not know your congregation ID number, please note:

Congregation: _____

Location: _____

Denomination: _____

Who prepared this evaluation?

Name: _____

I am: _____ Female _____ Male

I am: _____ Lay _____ Lay-rostered _____ Congregational pastor
_____ Pastor in specialized ministry/retired

I am: _____ Paid staff _____ Volunteer staff _____ Not staff

I am: _____ American Indian or Alaska Native
_____ Black or African American
_____ Hispanic or Latino/a
_____ Native Hawaiian or other Pacific Islander
_____ White
_____ Other: _____

I am: _____ Under 25 _____ 25–49 _____ 50–65 _____ over 65

Is this _____ a personal evaluation of the materials
_____ a response to which a group has agreed?

Have you been part of a group that studied or discussed these materials?

_____ Yes _____ No

What is the nature of this group?
_____ Congregation council or other congregational leadership
_____ Congregational study group made up primarily of lay people
_____ Group of congregational pastors and/or other rostered leaders
_____ Other (describe): _____

Please return the completed evaluation to:
ELCA—DCM
Attn: Renewing Worship Evaluation
8765 W. Higgins Rd.
Chicago, IL 60631

ISBN 0-8066-7007-X